Praise for *The Essential Advantage*

"Here, at last, is a book that helps a CEO sort through the many conflicting demands on him. Strategic opportunities and distracting temptation often look a lot alike. The framework that intrinsically links capabilities to strategy is clear; it makes sense; it's practical; and, I know from experience; it works."

—Al Daweesh, Group CEO of Saudi Telecom

"Companies have many strategic options, especially in fast-growing markets and industries. *The Essential Advantage* is a powerful reminder that capabilities should play the central role in sorting through them. Strategy should start with understanding what your company does really well—and using that knowledge to generate a corporate direction where you can be confident of winning."

—Ahmad Abdulkarim Julfar, Group Chief
Operating Officer, Etisalat Group

"This is a powerful book about strategy as choice. It demonstrates that coherence—treating your internal practices and your external business environment as interrelated and mutually focused—leads to competitive advantage. This path is not always easy to follow, but it will resonate at any company that is serious about its future."

—Ram Charan, coauthor of *The Game Changer*
(with A. G. Lafley) and author of
Boards That Deliver

"*The Essential Advantage* provides a pragmatic, holistic, and useful framework for understanding how to deliver performance. This straightforward read provides credible examples and a culmination of considerable thought and experience. There is no reason for competitive disadvantage, other than failing to deliver coherence."

—John Hofmeister, former President of
Shell Oil, CEO of Citizens for Affordable Energy, and author of
Why We Hate the Oil Companies

"*The Essential Advantage* picks up where most business books end. Rather than presenting an abstract treatise on capabilities-based strategy, the authors provide deep insights into what a capability is, the value of coherence among activities, and most importantly how executives can earn the right to win in their markets."

—Don Sull, Professor of Management Practice in
Strategic and International Management and
Faculty Director of Executive Education at
the London Business School

"*The Essential Advantage* sizzles. It is instantly useful in determining your organization's capabilities and how to make the most of them. Leinward and Mainardi use elegant, easy-to-follow models and compelling company stories to show what works and what doesn't in strategy. Using their exercises and terminology will give your organization a common footing and source of leverage."

—Karen Otazo, President, Global Leadership
Network, and author of *The Truth
About Being a Leader*

THE
ESSENTIAL
ADVANTAGE

Also by Paul Leinwand and Cesare Mainardi

Cut Costs and Grow Stronger: A Strategic Approach to What to Cut and What to Keep, an e-book

THE ESSENTIAL ADVANTAGE

HOW TO WIN WITH A CAPABILITIES-DRIVEN STRATEGY

PAUL LEINWAND

CESARE MAINARDI

Harvard Business Review Press
Boston, Massachusetts

Library of Congress Cataloging-in-Publication Data

Leinwand, Paul.
    The essential advantage : how to win with a capabilities-driven strategy / Paul
Leinwand, Cesare Mainardi.
        p. cm.
    ISBN 978-1-4221-3651-5 (hbk. : alk. paper)   1. Strategic planning.
2. Management.   3. Organizational effectiveness.   I. Mainardi, Cesare.
II. Title.
    HD30.28.L4493 2011
    658.4'012—dc22

                                                        2010022988

To those who taught us what is

essential in life.

CONTENTS

Contents

ACKNOWLEDGMENTS

To some extent, expressing appreciation to a few individuals who helped with this book misses the point: our perspective on value creation and strategy is derived from at least two generations of Booz & Company consultants who, over time, formed the fundamental ideas behind the capabilities-driven strategy. We especially thank our clients who collaborated with us to discover the essence of advantage. We admire them for their courage in embracing capabilities-driven strategies to boldly transform their companies.

But translating those ideas into this book took great focus and effort, and we must acknowledge those individuals who made it all happen.

Our firm's editor-in-chief, Art Kleiner—an amazing combination of leading business thinker and gifted storyteller—was our close partner throughout the process. It is difficult to properly express our gratitude to him for his vast contributions to this book; we know it certainly would not exist without him.

Our knowledge team at Booz & Company is world-class, and it is this group that energetically brings these concepts to life. Kate Pinkerton, the project's director, identified significant content while managing to organize the entire team to produce two books and a *Harvard Business Review* article within a year. Tom Stewart, our firm's chief knowledge and marketing officer, had insight into how these ideas would make a significant difference in the world of strategic thinking, and we thank him for encouraging and facilitating us. We had a first-class editing team supporting this project: Rob Hertzberg and Tara Owen enhanced the clarity of our ideas and helped us push further with their energy and enthusiasm.

There are so many colleagues at Booz & Company who have contributed to this book. Many of these individuals are highly regarded in their field, and their insights on the topic of strategy have been incredibly helpful. Thank you in particular to Gerald Adolph, DeAnne Aguirre, Jin Ahmed, Shumeet Banerji, Marty Bollinger, Niko Canner, Dave Coleman, Ivan de Souza, Niklas Eidmann, Ken Favaro, Alan Gemes, David Kantor, Per-Ola Karlsson, Jon Katzenbach, Nadia Kubis, Kenny Kurtzman, Steffen Lauster, Dan Lewis, Jack McGrath, Peter Mensing, Jan Miecznikowski, Amit Misra, Lisa Mitchell, Les Moeller, Marcus Morawietz, J. Neely, Gary Nelson, Karim Sabbagh, Samrat Sharma, Kolinjuwa Shriram, Ed Tse, Aurelie Viriot, and Dan West. They all devoted considerable time challenging our ideas, making them better, and helping us to review and improve the manuscript. An expert communications team helped to bring this book to the market; this includes Michael Bulger, Jon Gage, Sharon Harkey, Karen Henrie, Elizabeth Johnson, Frank Lentini, Penny Peters, Alan Shapiro, and Frank Sommerfield.

To our colleagues at Harvard Business Review Press, we learned what it meant to have a "value-added publisher," with your unending focus on improving the ideas. Thanks to Paul Michelman and Sarah Cliffe, who saw the potential of this project; to Melinda Merino, Jacque Murphy, Christina Bortz, and Erin Brown; and in particular to Ania Wieckowski, our editor for this book.

Judy Luczak and Debbie Page—who both would normally be thanked for keeping us organized—provided so much more support and thus gave us the freedom to think and write.

And most importantly, to our respective families and friends: you were supportive in every possible way. You encouraged us to take on this challenge, you sustained and guided us, and you accepted the time it took away from our personal lives. We return that time to you now, knowing that is what is most essential in life.

Chicago and Cleveland
July 13, 2010

I

STRATEGIC COHERENCE

CHAPTER ONE

THE ESSENCE OF ADVANTAGE

It's 8 a.m. in the executive conference room of a large global manufacturing company. About twenty-five people, most of them heads of businesses or of major functions, are seated around the table. A dozen more leaders are attending by phone, calling in from their respective regions. The occasion is a quarterly review of new growth options, and the head of one of the major business units is making her pitch now. Raised in Delhi, Aadya is a poised, fast-talking, 41-year-old engineer-turned-executive; she has been with the company ten years. Currently based in California, she spent much of this past year in India and other Asian countries, because that's where she believes the best prospects are for growth in their industry.

At the head of the table is the CEO, Martin—who, as it happens, hired Aadya when he was head of the North American business. He has been CEO for only four years, and already these meetings, which he initiated, have become a signature event in the company. It's a sign of status to be invited, because everyone knows that this is where the company's overall strategy is really hammered out.

Aadya is presenting an audacious new idea: an extremely inexpensive adaptation of one of the company's flagship devices, to be sold in emerging markets. If it works out, it won't just be mildly successful; hundreds of millions of people will purchase it.

Martin leans forward and asks Aadya a simple question: "Do we have the right to win in this business?"

People in the room have heard him ask this question before. But the calm, direct tone of his voice still makes most of them sit up a little straighter. It means something very specific. What makes Aadya so sure that they can compete effectively with this product? Has she chosen the right game to play? Do they have the right capabilities to deliver?

Martin's manner is reminiscent of a coach talking to an athlete: "Do you feel ready for this game?" Or a teacher asking a student: "Do you think you can ace this test?" But the stakes are much higher. The company could end up investing millions before anyone finds out whether the venture will succeed. The market could turn out to be much smaller than the company expects. An upstart competitor could knock off the device and underprice the company.

"Yes," Aadya says simply. She then carefully presents a logical analysis of the consumer market; a view of the competitors from a variety of countries, including India, China, and South Africa; and, most importantly, a detailed, sober, and well-considered view of the company's capabilities. The company is already skilled at procuring the materials it will need, and it has advanced marketing and distribution capabilities for reaching emerging-market consumers. Its innovation capabilities, on the other hand, would need to be expanded, particularly for creating simpler, lower-cost versions of their devices. Aadya thus proposes a new R&D technical center in Asia, which would find and develop local talent capable of doing this. She also quickly sketches out an acquisition plan that would provide the company with better access to some promising markets where it doesn't currently have a position. In all of this, she doesn't come across as trying to sell her idea, but as simply explaining the stakes and what it will take to make the proposal succeed.

When she's done, Martin leans back and laces his fingertips together thoughtfully. "I'm inclined to think we should do this," he says.

Aadya resumes breathing. She knows how few proposals ever get this far. But this is still not the full decision; it's an opening to a discussion.

A major question now needs to be answered by everyone: if the company makes this commitment, what will it take? What other capabilities—new and existing—will they need to support it? What investments would be required to bridge the gap? What savings will they need to find elsewhere to fund these investments? Around the table and on the phone, each person speaks in turn: regional leaders, functional directors, and the heads of other businesses, talking about the role they would have to play and the contribution they might make.

The conversation is relatively unforced and free of tension; this team has had many similar meetings, and everyone understands the types of growth ideas that will work and those that won't, given the company's capabilities profile. Two hours later, it is clear that the company is ready to stand behind Aadya's proposal. It will not be sent off to succeed or fail on its own; it will be an inherent part of the overall growth strategy, drawing on every major capability that the company has.

In a small but increasing number of companies, conversations like this are taking place today. They may not take this exact form, but the strategic relevance, the intensity, and the focused perspective on their business are the same. Companies like this are known to be consistently successful—to have an essential advantage that their competitors can't match. Sure, they make mistakes, sometimes huge ones. But more often than not, they learn from their errors and come back stronger. They focus their efforts on the products and services that succeed for them, and they continually and consciously reinvest in the capabilities that differentiate them the most. For all these reasons, their competitors have difficulty catching up.

These companies succeed, not because of what they own or how big they are or because they are positioned in the right industries. Their advantage lies in what they do and how everything fits together to create value. They succeed because they are coherent.

Why Coherence Matters

Coherence, to many people, means having your act together—acting with uniformity and coordination. In this book, coherence means something much more specific. For a company to be described as coherent, it must be resolutely focused and clear-minded about three critical elements: its market position (its chosen "way to play," if you will); its most distinctive capabilities, which work together as a system; and its product and service portfolio. In a coherent company, the right lineup of products and services naturally results from conscious choices about the capabilities needed for a deliberate way to play.

Achieving coherence with one, or even two, of these elements is not enough. Only when all three are in sync—with one another and with the right external markets—can a company truly claim the "right to win" in the contests that matter over time. This coherence generates the essential advantage that distinguishes leading companies. It is sustainable and almost impossible to copy—as opposed to being a transitory advantage that allows companies to thrive only for a while.

The essential advantage in business is coherence. Our core insight is that simple. To be sure, companies can enjoy other forms of business advantage—advantages based on products, brands, assets, or positions. But they are all transient. They are vulnerable to technological disruptions, upstart competition, and the shifting global economy. Patents and copyrights expire. Business processes prevail until more proficient competitors appear. Government protection erodes when policies change. Technological monopolies are threatened by new innovations.

At the same time, most organizations are "sticky": their identities, cultures, and relationships are by nature slow to adapt to changing conditions. You simply cannot adapt as rapidly and as often as the audience and technology around you. But by becoming more coherent, like a boat moving toward a lighthouse at night, you align your organization toward a clear, more visible, more constant goal. You are no longer as vulnerable to external events—or to your own internal fragmentation.

Consider your own struggles with incoherence. How many times have you followed a new strategic direction or pursued a new growth opportunity with an enormous investment of time and effort, but without creating much value? How many initiatives have you started that didn't fit with anything else in your company and that didn't achieve their desired results? How many conversations have you had, trying to balance the needs of multiple functions, businesses, and regions—each arrived-at solution reasonable in itself, but contradicting one another and overwhelming the budget and resources available to you?

"We're searching for the glue," lamented the CEO of one of the world's largest consumer products companies not long ago. He is not alone. Few senior executives spend enough time thinking about the enterprise as a whole. Incoherence has been a way of life in business for years. People are used to it. But it can no longer stand in today's business environment. Many companies are finding themselves forced to change.

To unlock the benefits of coherence, you need to take deliberate steps—to reconsider your current strategy, overcome the conventional separation between your outward-facing and inward-facing activities, and bring your organization into focus. In this book, we will show you how.

A Breakthrough Business in a Mature Market

To see what we mean by coherence, consider the story of the consumer health-care division of the pharmaceutical giant Pfizer, Inc. The division, which was big enough to be a *Fortune* 500 company in its own right, generated billions of dollars of value between 2002 and 2006. It did this by creating what some say is impossible: a breakthrough business in a largely mature market.

Most people know the division through its widely successful over-the-counter (OTC) pharmaceutical products: Listerine antiseptic mouthwashes, Benadryl and Zyrtec allergy medicines, Zantac heartburn relief aids, Sudafed cold remedies, Nicorette smoking cessation products, and Rogaine hair regrowth medications among them. These products came together under the Pfizer corporate roof through a series of acquisitions—chief among them the 2000 purchase of Warner-Lambert, a company that made a wide variety of medicines, candies, mints, and gums. Pfizer's main objective in the deal was attaining Lipitor, a prescription medicine for reducing cholesterol. Then, in 2002, Pfizer merged with another loosely configured company, Pharmacia, seeking its anti-arthritis medicine Celebrex and gaining other attractive pharmaceuticals as well.

When the dust cleared, Pfizer had a much greater presence and visibility in over-the-counter products than it had ever had before.

Because of these acquisitions, the company's annual OTC revenue leaped from $560 million to nearly $3 billion, and by merging and streamlining operations, the consumer health-care division successfully cut about $300 million in annual costs. But the leaders of this business faced a major challenge: they were not in the larger company's main-stream. They needed to convince the rest of Pfizer that nonprescription mouthwashes, pills, and ointments could represent a viable business with robust top-line growth.

Pfizer is a relatively decentralized company; its divisions operate with fairly high autonomy. The parent company has a tough, science-oriented culture, reflecting the medical background of its staff and leadership. Within this culture, Pfizer's consumer health-care division was a bit of an oddball. Though the head of business development, Tom Booth, had come from the pharmaceutical parent, most of the division's leaders, including its president, Marc Robinson, had spent their careers in Warner-Lambert, at the rough-and-tumble front lines of consumer product marketing. They all fit in well with the rest of Pfizer in one respect: they were ambitious. By 2002, they had renamed the division Pfizer Consumer Healthcare (PCH) and set out to build a comprehensive strategy for global growth, with the aim of seizing the number one position in consumer health care worldwide.

Robinson, Booth, and the rest of the top management team began by looking closely at the market dynamics in their over-the-counter business. At the time, this was a highly fragmented sector with low overall growth. No player enjoyed more than 5 percent share globally. One key avenue for expansion was the so-called Rx-to-OTC switch: converting prescription drugs (Rx) into less concentrated versions for sale without a prescription on a pharmacy or grocery shelf. But this process would require the ability to manage tight country-by-country health-care regulation. The changing worldwide demographics—aging populations, growing income levels, and faster-paced urban lifestyles—offered another opportunity and meant larger markets for self-medication. But it also meant more competition: mass retailers were gaining clout and introducing more private-label ("drugstore brand") versions of brand-name products.

Next, the PCH management team looked at what many conventional strategy experts would suggest: high-potential, unfulfilled, "adjacent" categories. Weight-loss products, for instance, had a huge potential market and no dominant over-the-counter offerings. But PCH had no offering, either, and there were many potential entrants with experience in marketing products related to behavioral change. Even if PCH invested heavily in R&D, there was no assurance that the division would find the solution (or that regulators would approve it). The division would have to grow by marketing its existing products more effectively.

The team members compared the growth rates in Pfizer's over-the-counter products with those of its competitors. To their surprise, in every category, one or two brands stood out from the pack. These included some of their competitors' products, such as Tylenol analgesics, Bayer aspirin, and Centrum vitamins, as well as Pfizer's own Listerine and Nicorette. The standouts were invariably the products that based their marketing on demonstrable health benefits. If a company had a better product that made consumers healthier and could make a claim about it—"Benadryl is 54 percent more effective than the leading prescription allergy medicine" or "Zantac works fast, right when you need it, even at night, when heartburn is worst"—it could build a thriving worldwide business even in historically low-growth categories (since the claim itself could attract new customers). The PCH team members thus realized something important: their proposition was less about retail marketing and more about health care than they had realized.

It took some courage to abandon a premise that had been ingrained in their thinking since the Warner-Lambert days: the old belief that in consumer health care, like foods and toiletries, winning the battle for category leadership (otherwise known as the battle for shelf space) determined success. But the president, Marc Robinson, had worked with claims-based advertising at Warner-Lambert; he understood the power of health-related marketing. Tom Booth, the head of business development, kept emphasizing the importance of a single strategy and disciplined choices. The team also had the example of Listerine, which had been sold as a cold and sore throat remedy in the United States until 1976, when the Federal Trade Commission had ruled against the claim. Sales had slackened thereafter until the late 1990s, when Listerine had introduced another claim: "Listerine reduces significantly more plaque than brushing or flossing alone." With this new claim, sales had rebounded. With the benefit of preventing gingivitis (and, later, of whitening teeth), Listerine didn't need line extensions like toothbrushes and toothpaste; PCH didn't need to try to dominate the whole oral-care shelf.

This realization gave the PCH executives confidence. Instead of competing through merchandising, they would bet on a few highly favored brands that provided a therapeutic benefit for consumers. PCH would make claims about them, have local regulatory authorities approve those claims, and take position accordingly. The products would solve simple health-related problems for people around the world.

The executives knew this strategy could be profitable, particularly since no other major consumer health-care producer conceived of its business in quite that way. But as they thought it through, they realized that to make their strategy actually work, PCH would have to become proficient—even world-class—in six capabilities. Three of them were existing core competencies for the Warner-Lambert side of the division:

- The launching and commercialization of new over-the-counter products, through Rx-to-OTC switches

- Claims-based marketing featuring a demonstrable health benefit (Warner-Lambert had already demonstrated this with Listerine, Sudafed, and other products)

- Effective retail execution (e.g., product positioning, claims communication, pricing, and promotion) in both general trade stores and pharmacies

Pfizer's people were already well versed in the other three capabilities:

- The ability to influence regulatory management and government policy (so that claims could stand in many countries and jurisdictions)

- Focused portfolio management of selected brands, to bring them to global scale

- The pharmaceutical-like innovation of new "forms and formulations" (as pharmacologists call their products), so that the company could raise the value of the products' health benefits

While each of these capabilities was important to fulfilling Pfizer's strategy, the way they fit together would be what differentiated the company competitively. To build an unbeatable franchise in claims-based marketing, Pfizer needed to ensure a steady stream of formulations about which to make those claims—hence the need for science-based innovation and robust Rx-to-OTC switching capabilities. The company needed the ability to get the claims approved by regulators and to translate this approval into terms that consumers world-wide could understand. It needed focused portfolio management of those few brands that promised blockbuster results, and focused retail execution, to ensure that anyone seeking a PCH remedy would feel assured that they could find it easily.

Having settled on this way to play and system of capabilities, the management team now looked at its portfolio of products. Some no longer fit. For example, personal care products (such as lotions and shaving cream) tend to sell according to fashion and personal preference. Success in this category has little to do with clinical evidence: a claim that a particular perfume or aftershave will help people smell "42 percent better," even if somehow provable, won't help the product's sales. Another broad category was confectionaries, such as Chiclets, Trident, and Bubblicious chewing gums. These products sell to impulse buyers; success requires rapid-cycle flavor innovation and the ability to command space in the front of the store near the cash register.

Though many of these brands were successful, Pfizer sold them. In 2003, Cadbury Schweppes bought its confectionary line and Energizer Holdings bought its Schick/Wilkinson Sword shaving products. The company focused its attention and resources on growing its handful of global "golden" brands (such as Listerine, Zyrtec, and Nicorette) while acquiring new brands such as Purell, which could also be differentiated based on claims: "Purell kills 99.99 percent of disease-causing germs within seconds."

During the next few years, PCH built a world-beating franchise in its blockbuster products in particular, making sure that the operational teams supporting its six capabilities worked seamlessly together in every market. (Chapter 11 describes some of the steps they took to accomplish this.) Very few other companies could have assembled this exact lineup of capabilities. Together, the Warner-Lambert and Pfizer legacy leaders created a strategy—as well as the proficiency and product line to back it up. For leaders and employees alike, one of the most rewarding aspects was the experience of being part of an enterprise where everything fit together and where they had earned a right to win in their chosen market.

By 2006, Pfizer Consumer Healthcare had grown its business to nearly $4 billion in annual sales. It was a premier business in its category, delivering a rate of growth that was double that of the industry.[1] The value of the division became even more evident in 2006, when Pfizer sold it to Johnson & Johnson for a price of $16.6 billion. This represented 20.6 times earnings (specifically, earnings before interest, taxes, depreciation, and amortization, or EBITDA), compared with average multiples of 15 at the time. Most of that remarkable purchase price represented the value created by the profitable growth engine that PCH had created.

The Three Elements of Coherence

The critical factor in PCH's success was clearly not the value of any particular brand or asset. Nor was it the division's continuously improving execution: strategist Michael Porter correctly dismisses what he calls "operational excellence" as insufficient in itself for success.[2] Nor was it, strictly speaking, the competitive position that PCH held. All of these were important, but the most significant factor was the division's ability to put it all together, to craft the pieces of strategy and execution into a workable and coherent system.

Pfizer did this by developing a trio of strategic elements that were interrelated. If you are a company seeking coherence, then you will get there by thinking through the same three elements for your own business (see figure 1-1).

1. A Way to Play: "How are we going to capture value in our market?"

Your company's *way to play* is your considered approach for creating and capturing value in a particular market, in a way that differentiates you from all other companies. A well-defined way to play is broad

FIGURE 1-1

A framework for coherence

Executives, managers, and employees at every level understand the way the company creates value for customers

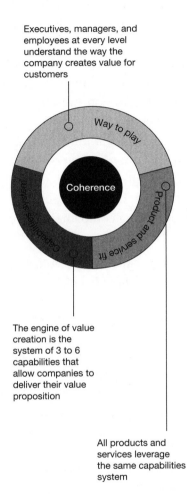

The engine of value creation is the system of 3 to 6 capabilities that allow companies to deliver their value proposition

All products and services leverage the same capabilities system

Source: Adapted from "The Coherence Premium," Paul Leinwand and Cesare Mainardi, *Harvard Business Review*, June 2010.

enough to allow flexibility and growth, but narrow enough to focus strategy and decision making. It may involve being an innovator, a low-cost provider, a premium player, or (more likely) a distinctive combination of strategic identities that fits your customers and capabilities precisely.

Pfizer Consumer Healthcare's way to play could be described in a sentence: "We provide solutions to simple health-related problems for consumers around the world, in non-prescription form, supported by verifiable and meaningful claims."

Your way to play is not chosen at random. It is determined through in-depth, relevant insight into your markets, and through an understanding of what you do uniquely well, namely, your capabilities. As we will see in chapter 4, the pattern of competition in an industry can be shaped by the ways that leading companies have chosen to play.

2. A Capabilities System: "What do we do with distinction to deliver this value?"

Your capabilities system is a combination of three to six mutually reinforcing activities that, together, allow you to fulfill your way to play. Each of the capabilities within this system is distinctive: it represents an extraordinary competence that few others can master. When deployed together, in a way that is relevant to your strategy, capabilities can enable your company to consistently outperform rivals. It's not just the assets you *have* that matter most; it's not even the products and services you *sell*. It's what you *do*, time and again, for the customers you serve.

These capabilities are not "table-stakes" activities like supply-chain management or sales—skills that every company must practice competently simply to be in business—or functions like human resources and finance. A capability, in this context, is the ability to reliably and consistently deliver a distinctive outcome, relevant to your business. This capability is ensured through the right combination of processes, tools, knowledge, skills, and organization, all focused on meeting the desired result.

Examples include the ability to secure shelf space in particular types of stores, to use customer-data mining to develop new products, to bundle products and services in a unique way, or to manage relationships with certain types of government authorities. It can take years to develop and refine the distinctive capabilities that set your company apart from others.

We are hardly the first to write about the importance of capabilities to strategy. C. K. Prahalad and Gary Hamel's seminal article, "The Core Competence of the Corporation," was published in 1990.[3] It was one in a long line of articles and books to make this point. But all too many businesspeople think of their capabilities as general functional areas, or as competencies created to match competitors, rather than as a mutually reinforcing system that drives strategy and value creation. London Business School professor Kim Warren thus deplores "the much-abused, misused and dangerous focus on 'core competences'—the idea that some unique and super-powerful capability will deliver sustainable competitive advantage."[4]

The full value of capabilities emerges only when they work together in a mutually reinforcing system linked to a viable way to play. The six PCH competencies, ranging from new product development to claims-based marketing to influencing regulators, comprise just such a capabilities system. Its value can't be attributed to any one capability but to the way they all work together. If your way to play represents a carefully chosen direction for your company, then your capabilities system is the engine that gets you there. We will take a closer look at capabilities systems in chapter 5.

3. Product and Service Fit: "What are we going to sell, and to whom?"

As a coherent company, you manage your portfolio so that every offering is supported by your unique capabilities system and aligned with your way to play. You remove products or services that require nonaligned capabilities. You might sell off divisions—even if they are profitable—if they would be worth more to other companies with a more appropriate way to play. You also scan the outside world for potential acquisitions of products and services that can take advantage of your own capabilities system.

The need for product and service fit explains Pfizer's divestitures of gum and razor blades and its acquisition of a hand sanitizer. Pfizer's sale of the PCH division to Johnson & Johnson was also, implicitly at least, based on this principle: that this capabilities system would be worth more to a maker of over-the-counter health products like J&J, which might apply such a system to all of its brands, than to a prescription-pharmaceuticals company like Pfizer with a single over-the-counter division. We'll discuss product and service fit further in chapter 6.

As we explore each of these elements more deeply in its own chapter, we will describe in detail how to define and develop them. The fundamental task of any effective business strategy is to bring these elements together: besides being market-sensitive and performance-conscious, your company also needs to be capabilities-driven.

The Capabilities-Driven Strategy

A capabilities-driven strategy is our name for the pragmatic series of choices that can lead you to increasing levels of coherence and therefore creates essential advantage. We prefer the phrase *capabilities-driven*, although other elements besides capabilities are involved, because the term recognizes the significant role that capabilities play as an engine of value creation.

As we'll see throughout this book, a capabilities-driven strategy is based on making stark choices about each of the three strategic elements in light of the other. Your way to play is derived not by the conventional approach of sizing a potential market for your products and services, but by an in-depth look at your current and potential customers, your possible opportunities for growth, your existing capabilities, and the ways they might evolve together. Your capabilities system is created according to the way you have chosen to play. Your lineup of products and services may have evolved over time in an ad hoc manner, but it is now going to be adjusted to correspond to the way you have chosen to play and the capabilities you can bring to bear. Your strategy is your judgment, continually honed through experience, about how to pull this all together.

It is also worth stating what a capabilities-driven strategy is *not*:

It is not focused on building capabilities for their own sake. It does not assume, as the movie *Field of Dreams* put it, that "if you build it, they will come." Capabilities must be integrated with one another and must support the company's overall way to play.

Nor does it focus (as strategy work often does) solely on external forces and trends, assuming that your company could rise to the challenge presented by any enticing market. You need to pick your challenges carefully: to play only the games that are not just worth winning, but that you know you can win.

It is not a prescription for narrow focus: for staying in one category, competing in one business sector, "sticking to your knitting," or selling just to one customer base. A coherent portfolio can be quite diverse, if it shares a system of unique capabilities.

It's not a portfolio, core competence, competitive analysis, or SWOT (strengths, weaknesses, opportunities, and threats) analysis. It is a fundamental logic for creating value, employing analytical techniques and other methods of sharpening and clarifying your judgment.

It is not bound by the customers you currently have; it looks explicitly for the customers you want to have.

A capabilities-driven strategy is not static. On the contrary, if you are clear-minded about how you create value, you have a better chance of adapting to new opportunities. You can shed old product lines and acquire new ones with confidence that they will succeed.

Nor is it purely adaptive and flexible, aimed at meeting any challenge even to the point of abandoning your consistent direction. It recognizes the value of the processes, practices, technologies, and habits that have taken you a long time to build.

It is not deterministic, proposing a single best way to succeed in any given industry. There are often several coherent strategies available for competitors; the more distinct they are from each other, the more viable they may be.

Finally, this type of strategy is not a formula for short-term results at the expense of long-term success. Companies with coherence tend to experience rapid improvement and growth spurts, but the goal is not a fast rise in profit figures. The goal is a sustainable, viable, ongoing creation of value.

The Context for Coherence

In our experience, companies setting out on the journey to greater coherence start in one of several situations. Some are in crisis. The bottom has dropped out of their business as a result of some disruptive external occurrence, their own missteps, or some combination of these, and the companies must overhaul their strategy.

Other firms have had success focusing on some of their businesses or divisions. Now they want to roll out the benefits of coherence in a more systematic, strategic way, and thus broaden that success to more of their enterprise.

Still others have been protected until now by circumstance—but they recognize that this protection is ending. They may be state-supported enterprises, have a patented technology or another asset, or enjoy a privileged position in a highly regulated economy. They may not have seen themselves as needing to compete on the basis of their capabilities at all, but now they face a transition to a more competitive world, and they need to prepare for it.

Another group of companies has been struggling to manage the increasing complexities of their business, squeezing by each year with cost reductions and modest growth estimates. These companies may have only recently recognized that their ordinary business approaches are no longer competitive, and they are exhausted from living incoherently. They are looking for a different path for growing stronger.

Finally, some companies have naturally tended toward coherence—and have, in the process, become models for others. Companies as varied as Apple, Inditex (the Spanish apparel company known for its Zara brand), Walmart, Amazon.com, the Finnish materials producer Ahlstrom, and the Brazilian bank Itaú Unibanco have all prospered by sticking to a well-considered way to play and applying their capabilities systems across a variety of products and services. But they know, as Intel CEO Andrew Grove famously put it, that "only the paranoid survive"—or, more precisely, that no matter how coherent you become, another more coherent rival can always appear.[5] They also know that coherence deteriorates over time unless it is continually cultivated and reinforced.

Maybe you are in one (or more) of these places. Or perhaps your situation is unique. Wherever you are starting from, you have one thing in common with all other companies: the historical context in which strategy is created today.

As Walter Kiechel points out in *The Lords of Strategy*, the idea of deliberately crafting a long-term focus and direction for a business is relatively recent.[6] It emerged in the 1960s, when leaders of large, mainstream companies began to analyze data on costs, prices, and operational expenses. Business strategies have evolved and shifted ever since then, with new prescriptions often compensating for the missing perspectives of their predecessors. Companies have tried to grow by building market share and economies of scale; by picking positions with high barriers to entry; by embracing execution and operational excellence; by seeking disruptive innovations and new markets; by developing their core competencies; by getting closer to their customers or adopting a more "market-back" orientation; by gaining more value from their existing businesses and assets; or by becoming more adaptive, fast-moving, and resilient.

All of these approaches (and many others) have merit. But they are generally regarded as prescriptions for a particular business problem or need, and thus they easily become disconnected in practice from any sustained, overall, strategic direction. It is not surprising that many companies, full of people trying to avoid failure and solve immediate problems, have adopted bits and pieces of all these approaches. In the process, they have moved down the path toward incoherence.

A capabilities-driven strategy represents an alternative direction: identify the underlying mechanism of value creation in your company (what you do best) and the opportunities for meeting the market effectively, and make a choice that fits them both together into a coherent strategic position.

How to Read This Book

Our views about coherence come from being strategy consultants in a firm that has worked with many companies during moments of crisis and business transformation. We've had a rare window on what allows organizations to establish and sustain success over time.

Together with our colleagues at Booz & Company, we began working on this type of strategy about fifteen years ago. Because we tend to stay with the same clients over many years, we saw the long-term results of their decisions, and we began to correlate the reasons for success or failure. We began testing our conclusions, both in analytic research (some of which is described in chapter 2) and more directly in practice. Gradually, we and our colleagues came to recognize how important coherence was.

The Essential Advantage is written for business leaders and other decision makers who recognize the benefits of coherence, but who haven't been able to realize its full strategic potential for their enterprise. If you are such a leader, we will show you how to move down the path to coherence: step-by-step, or all at once, at a pace your company can handle. And we'll show you how to reap both the rapid gains and the long-term growth and success that coherence brings with it.

In the chapters that follow, we articulate a capabilities-driven strategy process, explain how it creates value, describe the elements involved, and put them together step-by-step. At various points, we include short exercises that companies have found useful in bringing this type of strategy to life, in a "practical guide" format that you and your teams can work with.

In part I, we provide the fundamental logic for value creation and a road map for how your company can begin to develop and implement a capabilities-driven strategy. Chapter 2, "The Coherence Premium," explains in depth the rationale for this approach. It explicitly shows how coherence creates value for companies and, just as important, explains the penalties of incoherence. It draws on our research on the link between coherence and performance. We also examine some of the questions people have about the applicability of this strategy to mature industries, emerging markets (such as China and India), and companies with multiple large businesses (such as General Electric).

In chapter 3, "The Capabilities-Driven Strategy," we preview the journey that you and your management team undertake to develop the elements of strategy. You'll also learn how to assess your own current level of coherence.

Chapters 2 and 3 thus lay the groundwork for part II, which looks at the three components of your strategy as the variables in your strategic choices. Chapter 4, "The Way to Play," focuses on the nexus between your customers and your own capabilities. We show the difference a focused way to play can make in two well-known industries—consumer retail and personal computer manufacturing. We then show you how to research and settle on your own chosen way to play, starting with "puretone" ways to play that help you set your company's overall direction.

Chapter 5, "The Capabilities System," describes the relationship between capabilities and value creation and the impact that bringing together capabilities into a system can have. We recount one of the most remarkable capabilities system stories in business history, that of Amazon.com, and show how its example can be followed by companies in any industry.

Then in chapter 6, "Product and Service Fit," we introduce a more coherent way of thinking about your corporate portfolio. Describing the reinvention of a product lineup in a major materials producer (the Finnish company Ahlstrom) and a bold consumer product launch (Listerine PocketPaks), we explore the factors that allow particular businesses to thrive or fail. We then show you how to evaluate the parts of your company.

Part III explores some specific ways in which a company can create value coherently. Depending on how you manage them, your approaches toward growth, mergers and acquisitions (M&A), and cost-cutting will either reinforce or undermine your efforts to be coherent. Chapter 7, "Unlocking Growth," distinguishes coherent from incoherent ways of raising your top line. By distinguishing four different forms of growth—each with a different potential for coherence—we provide a launching point for thinking about more effective ways of expanding your business. We also describe one of the most common growth pitfalls: the "adjacency trap," illustrated by the remarkable story of the Anheuser-Busch and Frito-Lay snack food battle of the 1980s.

Chapter 8, "Mergers and Acquisitions," describes how to leverage coherence through mergers and acquisitions. By bringing a capabilities-driven strategy to bear, the genuine opportunities in M&A—not always visible from a conventional deal-maker's perspective—become more apparent. Here, too, we portray Amazon.com as a company to emulate.

Chapter 9, "Cut Costs and Grow Stronger," breaks through the long-standing presumption that costs and strategy are separate. In fact, in any successful movement toward coherence, the mastery of costs is extremely important. We show how two companies—Johnson Controls International and the R.J. Reynolds tobacco company—made sure that a crisis in their business did not go to waste.

Part IV, the final section, describes how to live coherence every day, with the reorganization and revitalization of your company at center stage. Chapter 10, "The Essential Advantage Roadmap," is a practical, step-by-step guide to the analyses, conversations, and choices in a capabilities-driven strategy development.

Chapter 11, "Organizing for Coherence," describes the organizational changes, informal practices, and talent-related approaches that enable a company to bring a capabilities-driven strategy to fruition.

Chapter 12, "The Capable Leader," is a brief evocation of the role of the chief executive. The pursuit of essential advantage is powerfully rewarding. But it requires courage to make the necessary choices, and stamina and skill to execute them.

In the end, a coherent, capabilities-driven strategy is not just a direction for future activity. It is a statement about the way that your enterprise creates value now and can create more value in the future. Every company has at least one potential breakthrough business available to it. You don't luck into realizing this potential. It is your strategic imperative to discern it, define it, and deliver it.

A GLOSSARY OF THE ESSENTIAL ADVANTAGE

Several terms are particularly useful in describing these concepts and are used throughout the book. They are defined below.

Coherence: A resolute, clear-minded focus in a company on three critical elements: its way to play, its most distinctive capabilities, and its lineup of products and services. The better aligned these three elements, the more coherent the company. Coherence can be estimated by assessing the extent to which a company's products and services share the same distinctive capabilities.

Relative coherence: Your company's degree of coherence compared with competitors', and a strong indicator of higher performance and comparative success.

Capability: The ability to reliably and consistently deliver a specified outcome, relevant to your business (i.e., in support of your way to play). This capability is ensured through the right combination of processes, tools, knowledge, skills, and organization, all focused on meeting the desired result. The most important capabilities are distinctive: each of them represents an extraordinary competence that few others can master.

Capabilities-driven strategy: A pragmatic series of choices that is designed to lead you to increasing levels of coherence and thus creates an essential advantage for your company over time.

Way to play: A considered approach for creating and capturing value in a particular market, in a way that differentiates a company.

Capabilities system: A group of three to six mutually reinforcing distinctive capabilities, organized to support a particular way to play.

Product and service fit: The degree to which your lineup of products and services is supported by your unique capabilities system and aligned with your way to play.

Value: The enterprise value of a company, reflecting the ongoing willingness of customers to purchase the products and services the company offers. Coherence provides a company with reliable and sustainable ways of generating value.

Essential advantage: An ingrained ability to succeed that distinguishes leading companies, is sustained over time, and is almost impossible to copy—as opposed to a transitory advantage, which allows companies to thrive only for a while.

Right to win: The confidence held by companies with an essential advantage, recognizing that they are better prepared than their competitors to attract and keep the customers they care about.

CHAPTER TWO

THE COHERENCE PREMIUM

Nearly every senior executive we talk to agrees that coherence is critically important. And yet companies everywhere are drowning in incoherence.

This is most evident when you look at the ways most companies set their priorities. Down from the senior executive team come financial targets intended to improve results. Each directive is well-intentioned and would be reasonable in itself, especially if the business units had a way to play that could guide them or a capabilities system that could deliver. But together, they often add up to an expectation of "surprise and delight" performance that is impossible to fulfill.

Faced with that expectation, business unit leaders do the only thing they can. They pick their objectives for growth with the most rapid probable returns, while nipping at whatever costs they find. They also demand the capabilities they need from functions like IT, human resources, R&D, and operations, to meet all the clashing imperatives they face.

Because these requests are disparate, and not driven from the company's way to play, the priorities seem vague: "We need to be better in consumer insights," or "We should be best in innovation." There is no common view of what type of insights or innovation is truly important for the business.

The functional leaders try as best as they can to meet as many of the businesses' needs as possible. They either distribute their limited investment and resources or request new investment to help them respond to new requests. Either way, this results in the company being "OK at everything, great at nothing."

To manage the many deserving proposals they receive, top executives fall into the role of budgetary referee. In normal times, all the players get some portion of what they ask for. In bad times, everybody is cut nearly the same percentage, across the board. No group receives the full investment it needs to be distinctive. Nor is there any discussion about making the most of the resources available. Thus, many resources are either ill used or wasted outright. Some managers learn to take the proposals that don't get funded and to resubmit them with a higher estimate of success. The company thus funds proposals that don't fit its goals, and launches projects without giving them the wherewithal to follow through. The capabilities most relevant for strategic success are easy to sacrifice or shortchange, because there is little agreement about which of them are essential.

These problems with poorly used or wasted resources add up to what we call the *incoherence penalty*. It is all the more pernicious because it is frequently unrecognized as the source of poor performance. But it is apparent if you look for it.

You can hear the incoherence penalty, for instance, in the frustration voiced quietly by business unit and functional leaders. The head of a division or product line says, "I could do so much more if senior management stopped meddling and let me make more decisions." The heads of operations, IT, human resources, and other functions complain, "I could deliver so much more if everybody sat down and agreed to set priorities." But the underlying problem isn't meddling, and consensus won't make much difference unless the strategic logic of the business is sound. The root cause is a lack of coherence around the company's strategy. Until this is dealt with, no organizational or cultural solution can possibly resolve the inherent conflict present in every decision.

Quarter after quarter, the lack of coherence generates poor results, which lead to even more pressure on performance and therefore more unrealistic expectations, more quick cuts, more inappropriate growth moves, and even poorer results. Eventually, time runs out. Management is changed, the company may be restructured or sold, and the vicious cycle starts all over.

Fortunately, as we'll show in this chapter, the incoherence penalty can be reversed into a virtuous cycle. A deliberate, coherent strategy leads to more effective use of resources, to more powerful capabilities, and to greater returns, which reaffirm the value of a more coherent strategy.

We call this the *coherence premium*. While less prevalent than the incoherence penalty, it is just as recognizable. It manifests itself in very tangible ways: shareholder value, growth, operating margin, and a confident, optimistic corporate culture.

Tracking the Coherence Premium

We have tracked the coherence premium in several industries, and the relationship between coherence and performance appears consistently. For example, an analysis of the consumer packaged-goods industry over five years of recent business history shows a clear link between coherence and financial returns (see figure 2-1).

The figure plots financial performance against coherence for fourteen major consumer-products companies. The y-axis shows financial performance, as measured in EBIT margin (earnings before interest and taxes, divided by net revenue). Similar correlations exist between coherence and shareholder value, though EBIT margins are more easily comparable across long periods of time.

On the x-axis, we rank companies according to a capabilities coherence score. This is based on the degree to which critical capabilities are shared across a company's products and services. We obtained this score through a sequence of steps:

1. Identify relevant general capabilities (in this sector, they included rapid flavor innovation, in-store execution, etc.) for the companies being studied.

FIGURE 2-1

The coherence premium in consumer packaged goods, 2003–2007

*An in-depth analysis of the consumer packaged-goods industry shows a clear correla-
tion between coherence and financial performance. The size of the circles indicate
relative 12-month revenue at the time of the study.*

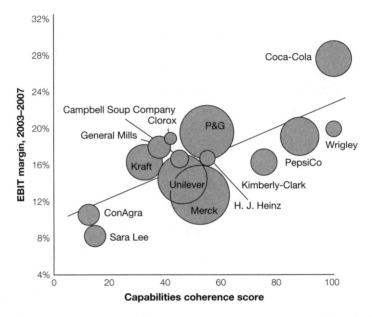

Source: Reprinted from Paul Leinwand and Cesare Mainardi, "The Coherence Premium," *Harvard Business
Review*, June 2010.

2. Break each company's portfolio into distinct business segments
   (prepared meals, personal care, toys and games, candy and
   confectionaries, etc.).

3. Determine (through public information and proprietary knowledge) the relative importance of each capability to each business
   segment.

We based each company's coherence score on how much that company's capabilities varied in importance from business segment to
business segment. If capabilities were important to most or all segments, the company ranked high; if most business segments had different capability requirements, the company ranked low. The scores

were statistically adjusted for revenue, variations in segment size, and complexities related to international operations or other confounding factors. Although this formula doesn't necessarily reflect the specific choices a company might make in its own capabilities-driven strategy, the score provides a reasonable proxy as seen from the outside.

The correlation is clear. The greater the coherence—the more market segments sharing the same critical capabilities—the greater the profitability. No matter how large or small the company, this correlation holds.

The standout performer is The Coca-Cola Company. This company is remarkably coherent, even compared with formidable (and relatively coherent) competitors like PepsiCo, Inc. All of the company's beverages—carbonated soft drinks, sports drinks, health drinks, energy drinks, juices, teas, and coffees—rely on the same three key capabilities.[1] The first is brand proposition: advertising and promoting some of the most ubiquitous and iconic product identities in the world. The second is store distribution, always a key focus and often direct to the store; Coca-Cola has a highly refined sales, merchandising, and delivery capability that enables it to execute at the retail level more effectively than its beverage competitors. This capability is linked to its third (and distinctively powerful) capability in franchising: overseeing and managing a global network of bottlers and distributors.

Together, these capabilities enable Coca-Cola to attract billions of people in more than two hundred countries. The company succeeds by building demand for products that only "The Coca-Cola System" (as it is called within the company) can deliver around the world. At times, Coca-Cola has flirted with businesses that don't fit its strategy. For example, it purchased Columbia Pictures in 1982, but sold it to Sony just seven years later. The Coca-Cola Company always returns to The Coca-Cola System.

On this continuum, other relatively coherent companies with higher-than-average performance include Pepsi and the capabilities system of its subsidiary Frito-Lay; Wrigley, the gum-maker recently acquired by Mars, Inc.; and Kimberly-Clark, makers of disposable diapers, tissues, and other paper products. We will discuss these companies and their coherence strategies later in this book.

Then there's Procter & Gamble. The position of this eminent consumer packaged-goods company in the center of figure 2-1 represents an average of its remarkable movement from the lower left to the upper right of the continuum in just over eight years. In early 2000, when A. G. Lafley assumed the CEO role, P&G's stock price was falling, a decline attributed generally to an ambitious but failed expansion drive during the late 1990s. (Lafley's appointment, then regarded as the elevation of a relatively young and inexperienced company insider, exacerbated the decline at first.[2]) At that time, P&G made and sold products in a variety of categories: diapers, laundry and cleaning products, health and beauty, feminine care, snack foods (Jif peanut butter, Crisco oil products, and Pringles potato chips), beverages (Folgers coffee and SunnyD drinks), food ingredients (Olestra), heat compresses (ThermaCare), and pharmaceuticals (such as the osteoporosis medicine Actonel).

P&G's products might have succeeded more if they had all fit with the renowned capabilities system that it had spent decades developing. One component of that system was a world-class, technology-based innovation capability aimed at providing reasonably priced, life-enhancing or life-changing products that could be sold around the world. (Crest Whitestrips teeth whiteners and the popular Swiffer mop are two recent examples.) P&G also had a powerful international marketing capability, reaching consumers in many countries who were all attracted to the same types of benefits. This capabilities system formed the basis of a highly consistent global consumer-product machine, lining up perfectly behind iconic brands such as Crest, Tide, and Pampers.

But the system was not a natural fit with all the products in P&G's portfolio. For example, highly innovative foods and beverages could not, over time, easily hold their own in a category dominated by merchandisers that pushed out more flavors to more supermarket shelves in a lower-cost model. This was true even of Pringles, where their capabilities system had developed the innovative and consistently shaped "potato chips in a can" with an army of loyal devotees. Moreover, tastes in snacks and beverages tend to vary from one region to the next, so P&G's global marketing model wasn't always as effective as it was in non-food categories, especially against competitors who could more easily adjust their packaging, flavoring, and messaging to match local markets. Most importantly, while P&G's product lines tended to be strong competitors individually, the differences among them made the company relatively incoherent as an organization, and that dragged down its advantage. As Lafley later recalled, "[P&G's] people were not oriented to any common strategic purpose."[3] His job, he said, was to decide what business P&G was in—and what it was not in.[4]

Under Lafley and his successor, Robert McDonald, P&G sold off most of the products that would be better supported by other capabilities systems. These included its pharmaceutical division and most of its food divisions, even though some of these were performing well at the time. Lafley and his executive team then focused on strengthening P&G's most important capabilities: for example, boosting its R&D effectiveness with open-innovation initiatives that allowed the company to draw on ideas from all over the world. They also focused on developing or acquiring product segments that would benefit from the company's distinctive capabilities—for instance, by purchasing Gillette in 2005. P&G's stock price has tripled since 2000; the commercial success rate for new products now runs between 50 and 60 percent (compared with 15 percent in 2000); and Lafley, the "inexperienced insider," was recognized for his management insight in a variety of venues, including being named executive of the year by the Academy of Management in 2007.[5]

Down at the bottom left of the coherence spectrum reside ConAgra and Sara Lee, and a quick scan of their product portfolios indicates why. Because both companies have complex portfolios assembled through decades of acquisitions, the businesses require a wide range of capabilities in support. For example, during the earlier years covered by this analysis, Sara Lee's product lines comprised its own branded baked goods, Ball Park hot dogs, Hanes underwear, Kiwi shoe polish, Brylcreem hair care products, Coach luggage, Best's kosher meats, a variety of food service operations, and many other product lines. Sara Lee historically applied a highly decentralized management model to manage all this and thus employed a wide range of capabilities. The food and beverage categories required various forms of product formulation, packaging, sourcing, and supply-chain prowess, while the company's household and personal care products deployed entirely different operational, marketing, and distribution capabilities. To add a further level of complexity, the company's product line varied by geography. All of this has been reflected in the company's relatively low financial performance.

Under the leadership of Brenda Barnes, who became CEO in 2005, Sara Lee has begun to seek more of a coherence premium.[6] The company has focused its attention on branded meats, food services, coffee, and baked goods, spinning off most of its other businesses and developing strategies based on deploying common capabilities for its products within each category.[7]

You might conclude from this that being a large corporation with a single-category high-margin product line, like The Coca-Cola Company, is the key to having a high coherence score—and hence to success—but the analysis shows that the benefits of capability coherence are not limited to this kind of scale. Small players such as Wrigley (before its 2008 acquisition by Mars) and complex players like P&G also have high coherence scores. In general, factors like size, scale, and even the number of products and services matter less than the company's choices about the three strategic elements.

An analysis of the automobile industry over a comparable eight-year period produced similar results. Here again, when capabilities were matched with car brands and segments, the companies with the most consistently applicable attributes—Porsche, BMW, Toyota, and Honda—were also the best financial performers.

The same correlation also holds true for other industries, such as financial services, telecommunications, and health care. In every test we have conducted so far, there is a coherence premium, and the premium accrues to any company that moves along the continuum to align its way to play, capabilities system, and product and service fit.

To learn more about, or participate in, our ongoing
research on this subject, visit
www.theessentialadvantage.com.

Four Sources of Value

Why is coherence essential to sustained performance for your company? How does it produce the benefits that we saw in a variety of industries? We have found four specific, observable ways in which coherence generates value: effectiveness, efficiency, focused investment, and alignment.

Effectiveness

One consistent effect of a capabilities-driven strategy is renewed emphasis on, and continuous improvement of, the most relevant capabilities. Day in and day out, you become more effective where it matters most. You "sweat" your capabilities, refining and developing your methods and processes. Because your capabilities reinforce one another in a system, they improve more rapidly than those of your more scattered competitors. Not only do you gain in operational excellence, but you also become more skilled at making the right choices. In a competitive environment, this gives you an increasing edge; as you advance, other companies find it more and more difficult to catch up.[8]

Becoming more effective is a key component of your company's right to win against competitors. Your people become more skilled; your systems grow more adept; your profitability improves. Customers are attracted to you because of this added value for them, so your share of the market increases as well. Sooner or later, this leads to a second-order gain in effectiveness: success accrues to the successful. As you become perceived as a market leader and a source of excellence, you attract more and better customers, business partners, employees, leaders, and long-term investors. With all of these to draw on and learn from, your capabilities improve even more. This creates a lock on value that is enormously difficult for competitors to replicate.

Efficiency

As you apply your capabilities more broadly across more products and services, you get more value out of them. Your investment in each of them goes further. You can afford to hire a team of specialists in online marketing, to recruit a senior vice president who really knows the health industry, or to build a state-of-the-art supply chain, because the costs of building capabilities, which can be very high, are amortized across your entire portfolio. Small parts of your business, which could never afford these capabilities if they were separate, can take advantage of them with you.

Depending on your way to play, your ability to deploy capabilities at a lower cost can provide a pricing advantage, catalyze higher margins, or enable you to invest more in these important capabilities. There is far less duplication of effort as well; you're less likely to have different business units installing separate IT systems because they each need different features. Meanwhile, your less coherent competitors must bear the expense of disparate capabilities for every one of their offerings.

Focused Investment

A coherent system makes the most efficient use of your resources, attention, and time. You spend the most where you need the most. By allocating capital and expense more deliberately and effectively, you focus more on the capabilities that differentiate your company competitively and less on what Gary Hamel and C. K. Prahalad called "table stakes"—the necessary competencies and skills that every competitor brings to this market.[9] Moreover, you avoid the expense of investments that breed incoherence. You don't, for example, make accounts payable world-class; you don't fund unnecessary R&D projects or marketing campaigns. You invest in depth where depth is needed, and go light where you should go light.

Here, too, a virtuous cycle kicks in. As your company's staff become more aware of the impact of focused investment on growth, they become more motivated to participate. We have seen R&D meetings, for example, where the project leaders get excited about a particular idea. Then someone says, "Hang on. That won't thrive in our capabilities system," and the company avoids the time and expense of considering an incoherent funding request. Meanwhile, ideas that might have been overlooked or discarded, but that fit the company's strategy, can get their moment in the sun.

Alignment

When you commit to a strategy and articulate it clearly, then everyone has a common basis for the day-to-day decisions they make. Throughout your company, people in different businesses and different geographic areas are attuned to the same capabilities system and way to play. They are thus more likely to understand one another, and to make independent decisions that are nevertheless in sync. They combine forces and share resources more easily. They execute faster and with more force, because they are not held back by concern about what their colleagues might think. More coherent decision-making becomes part of your company's culture. The advantage this gives you over smaller-scale or less coherent competitors is palpable.

One often-unexpected result is the ease of attracting and retaining high-quality talent in professions related to your capabilities system. These highly skilled people—be they engineers, traders, researchers, analysts, designers, lawyers, physicians, or specialists of any sort—will find opportunities in your company across a wide range of products, services, businesses, and parts of the world. This means they will have more opportunity for advancement, more recognition within the company, many opportunities to practice their craft, a large network of peers, and the enhanced reputation and day-to-day fulfillment that comes from all of these factors. Recruiters and candidates know this, and the best people in the most relevant fields will be drawn to work for or with you.

All four of these sources of value reinforce one another. Alignment makes it easier to integrate people across the company, which leads to greater effectiveness as people learn from their colleagues. An ethic of careful investment leads people to find ways to use their capabilities in more parts of the organization. Before too long, your company can grow at a faster pace, and at lower cost, than it ever could before.

Absolute and Relative Coherence

How much will your company have to change to experience these benefits? That depends, of course, on how coherent you already are. Unquestionably, a company that ruthlessly looks at its business, aligns everything closely to a focused and powerful capabilities system, and divests the products and services that don't fit will start to see the coherence premium kick in very quickly.

But you do not have to go that far. In many cases, it may be unrealistic to try. To realize the value of the coherence premium, you simply need to be relatively coherent: to align your way to play, capabilities system, and lineup of products and services better than your competitors do. In any given industry, with all other circumstances being relatively equal, a more coherent company generally outperforms a less coherent one.

The key is to make hard choices about the elements in your system. It is very difficult to develop three or four, let alone six, truly differentiating capabilities. More than six, in our view, is probably unworkable. Prahalad and Hamel came to a similar conclusion: "Few companies are likely to build world leadership in more than five or six fundamental competencies," they wrote.[10] Similarly, while some companies deliberately develop two ways to play, with capabilities systems to match, this is a more expensive and distracting path, with less of a coherence premium, than focusing on one.

You do not need to commit everything to a single way to play immediately. Road blocks and realities may make a single focus impractical, particularly in the short term. Again, there is great value in relative coherence. If you have two or three ways to play, each with its own capabilities system, and your products and services are lined up accordingly, you will have a great advantage over competitors with ten or fifteen separate and unrelated businesses and no common capabilities system at all.

Is Coherence Right for Everyone?

As we explored the value of coherence, we found four types of conceptual challenges—concerns raised about the applicability of this approach to every type of company. Some question the value of coherence in a struggling industry, like airlines or chemicals. Others argue that in a global environment, where companies must operate in many geographic locations, a single way to play and capabilities system cannot apply. The third group, typically thinking of emerging markets, wonders if the idea of capabilities applies to places where the dynamics of government involvement and competition are distinctively different from the more mature economies of the West. The fourth argument raises the experience of conglomerates: are there not companies that can manage multiple businesses, with multiple ways to play, more effectively than their single-business counterparts?

These four arguments are similar, in our view, because they reflect an implicit assumption that the complex trade-offs in business today are unresolvable. Many businesspeople assume that they must live with the limits of incoherence: in their industry, their geographic locations, or their own company. To us, these seeming limits are really signals of strategic opportunity. If your company is wrestling with incoherence in its geographic expansion or its mix of products and services, then chances are your competitors are as well. By marshaling a capabilities-driven strategy and moving toward coherence, you may have a chance to move past the constraints that have, up until now, defined the way your business or industry operates.

Let's look at these four arguments in more detail.

Troubled Industries

Many managers have taken to heart Michael Porter's admonition about the relationship between the competitive structure of an industry and the profitability of companies within it. If the forces shaping industry structure "are intense," he wrote, "as they are in such industries as airlines, textiles, and hotels, almost no company earns attractive returns on investment. If the forces are benign, as they are in industries, such as software, soft drinks, and toiletries, many companies are profitable."[11]

Though Porter took pains to explain that industry structures can change and can be shaped by the actions of leading companies, he has often been interpreted as saying that some industries are innately good, while others are irredeemably bad. If you're in a tough business—or, conversely, if you're in a protected industry, like electric power, which in many countries is isolated from ordinary economic realities—then there's no real advantage to having a distinctive way to play or capabilities system.

Yet look more closely at the airline industry, a field bedeviled by high operating and labor costs, varied global regulation, oscillating fuel prices, and high vulnerability to storms, natural disasters, and terrorism. Who could make money in that business? Nonetheless, a study of publicly held airlines in 2009 found twenty with reasonable levels of financial health. Ryanair, Singapore Airlines, easyJet, AirAsia, and Southwest Airlines were at the top of the list.[12] Southwest Airlines, Ryanair, and Singapore Airlines, in particular, are known for their distinctive, well-matched systems of capabilities. They don't do things that don't fit their way to play. Similarly, in the 1980s, steel and aluminum were considered inherently cyclical businesses, doomed to debilitating downturns—until Nucor, with its minimills, and Alcoa under Paul O'Neill, proved otherwise. In short, even in a competitively intense industry, you can find a coherent strategy that causes enough differentiation that you can create a high level of value.

To be sure, many businesspeople see these cases as outliers—as rogue companies that somehow escaped the strictures of a bad industry. But from a coherence perspective, these companies found effective ways to play that didn't just escape industry dynamics, but also changed them. Increased coherence often creates value by changing the industry structure. Over time, through mergers and acquisitions (including the acquisition of failed competitors), products and brands often migrate to the companies with the capabilities best equipped for them—typically the companies willing to pay the greatest acquisition premiums for products and services that fit. As they differentiate themselves, the most coherent companies take dominant positions, and customers migrate to them—leading to more sustained advantage for clearly differentiated competitors.

That is what happened in the diaper wars, a well-known marketing battle of the consumer products industry. Starting in the late 1970s, there were two leading producers of disposable diapers. Procter & Gamble, which invented Pampers disposable diapers and launched them in 1961, and Kimberly-Clark, which entered the category with Kimbies in 1968, launched its better-selling Huggies brand in 1978 and became the market leader in the early 1980s. The two firms competed fiercely on both price and such innovations as fasteners, increased thinness, leak guards, and fit improvements. This provided consumers with great performance and value, at ever-lower prices, but it also limited the profitability of the category.

As time went on, however, the two companies began to differentiate, starting with their technology. Disposable diapers are remarkably complex, highly engineered products, combing advanced adhesives,

38

waste-treatment chemicals, and the layering of paper, plastic, and cellulose pulp. The diapers must hug the infant, absorb human waste, draw it away from the skin, mask the smell, prevent leaks, fit under clothes, and promote health and comfort.[13] Both companies assured consumers that they had all these features, but each emphasized different qualities in the final product. Thus Procter & Gamble's way to play focused on claims that its diapers prevented more leaks and unwanted accidents. This was backed up by the company's solid capabilities system: its prowess in technology and global marketing. Kimberly-Clark was more of an experience provider; it offered a more emotional connection to mothers with a different marketing message, distributed through more media channels, emphasizing the diaper's remarkable fit, sizing system, and reputation for comfort.

As P&G and K-C deployed their different technological and marketing capabilities, the two sets of attributes, increasingly distinct, attracted different customers. A third group of customers, the most cost-conscious purchasers, drifted to private-label store brands. Gradually, the price wars abated; though the segment remains highly competitive, profitability for both P&G and K-C improved. Without collusion, the sector evolved, driven by differences in ways to play and capabilities systems.

Something similar may be happening right now in the specialty chemicals industry—the makers of the ingredients in such products as inks, coatings, paints, and solvents. Since the mid-1980s, like the chemicals industry in general, this group of companies has faced maturing markets, increasing commoditization, more demanding customers, new competitors (currently emerging in the Middle East and China), and a diminishing pipeline of new products as the innovation rate in the chemical sector has generally declined. In this environment, it has sometimes seemed as if there is no option but to compete on price, with lower margins and less investment in R&D.

But it's now becoming clear that there are several ways to compete. Some businesses, like Reliance Industries and LyondellBasel Industries, are low-cost value players, producing bulk chemicals to be delivered in quantity. Others are customizers: they tailor their existing products for individual customers in particular industries, helping them solve particular problems—for example, making paints and coatings to the specifications of particular automakers, or thermoplastic-enhanced compounds for aerospace companies. A third group is basing their business on customer-centric innovation: designing new "solutions and materials," as they call it, specifically to fit the individual needs of their manufacturer customers.

Each of these ways to play requires a very different capabilities system. For example, in purchasing GE Plastics, SABIC (Saudi Basic Industries Corporation) has been forced to move from being purely a value player to also operating as a customizer (and a solutions provider in some segments). In some cases, this means significant change or major new investment. But the specialty chemical companies that focus on these ways to play, rather than looking for business wherever they can find it, are beginning to generate better returns; the industry's customers are migrating accordingly, and the overall structure of the industry appears to be changing to reflect those ways to play.[14]

Multiple Geographic Areas

A commonly held belief in mainstream business is that global expansion is not only attractive (particularly in capturing the high growth rates of emerging markets), but also required. After all, that is how companies gain scale. But as IESE Business School professor Pankaj Ghemawat points out in *Redefining Global Strategy*, many companies have lost a great deal of value by proceeding as if "borders don't matter . . . [They are] most likely to compete internationally the same way that [they] do at home."[15]

We agree with Ghemawat that the world is in a state of *semi-globalization*. In other words, although communications, finance, and transportation links have made the world "flatter" than it used to be, the differences from one country to the next are still formidable. Even within regions, such as Western Europe or the Middle East, there are great differences in culture, labor relations, access to labor, government policy, and infrastructure (including distribution channels) from one country to the next. Your ability to manage these factors depends, in part, on the capabilities demanded by the conditions in a given locale. A telecommunications company, for example, depends on local landline infrastructure and is governed by strict regulation. It requires different capabilities when those factors vary, as they often do between countries. For all these reasons, your way to play in some geographic areas may be incompatible with other areas.

Nonetheless, this doesn't mean that you should apply a different way to play and capabilities system everywhere. Companies that develop a geographic strategy based on coherence—expanding where their capabilities system applies—have a natural advantage. Some of the first companies to master this in emerging markets, for example, are the "new blue chips," businesses that start in one emerging region and become global powerhouses elsewhere by drawing on the capabilities systems that they mastered in their home countries.[16]

Gruma SA, a company headquartered near Monterrey, Mexico, typifies this group. In Mexico, Gruma produces corn flour and related products, but around the world, it uses its capability in food processing—the ability to roll any kind of flour into salable flatbread—to great advantage. The company sells corn tortillas in Latin America, *naan* in India and the United Kingdom, and rice wraps in Beijing. In 2006, Gruma invested $100 million in a new Shanghai manufacturing plant, selling flatbread to Japan, Korea, Singapore, Thailand, the Philippines, and China.

"In the first stage," said Gruma chairman Roberto Gonzalez Barrera, "we will supply the continental China market, gradually increasing our range to the European and Asian borders of the Middle East. To us, this is a long-term investment that will lead to strategic new business opportunities."[17] As we'll see in chapter 7, this focus on capabilities (in Gruma's case, advanced manufacturing and marketing of flour and flatbread) provides a much better vehicle of expansion than more conventional "adjacency" moves, such as producing frozen meals that use tortillas. Those would require vastly different capabilities.

The Beijing-based Li Ning athletic shoe and apparel company provides another example of a company parleying distinctive capabilities into a carefully tailored geographic expansion. The company was founded by its namesake, Li Ning, a very famous Chinese Olympic gold medalist in gymnastics. It based its first moves out of China, into France and Argentina, on the capabilities deliberately built up by its founder for the Chinese market: rapid product introductions; inexpensive manufacturing; fast-follower design; and audaciously competitive, sports-related marketing (with a special emphasis on team sponsorships in countries outside China, including basketball in Argentina, Spain, and the United States). The company's most visible marketing coup occurred at the 2008 Summer Olympics in China, when Li Ning himself lit the torch at the opening ceremony. Though the company was not a sponsor of the games, its name was heard around the world when he was introduced as its founder—a blow to Adidas, which had spent hundreds of millions on Olympics-related sponsorship and marketing. Then in 2010, the company opened its first American store, choosing Portland, Oregon—Nike's home turf—as the location.[18]

Another example from China is Huawei, one of the world's leading telecommunications equipment manufacturers and network services providers. Founded in 1988 to serve Chinese markets only, it expanded geographically after 1996, starting with Hong Kong. By 2004, most of its revenues came from outside China. Huawei started out producing switches and routers that were considered "just good enough" technologically for emerging markets, but they were inexpensive, up-to-date, and brought to market rapidly. Over the years, as Huawei increased the quality of its equipment and entered more industrialized countries, it still kept prices low and operated as a value player. Although this way to play sometimes led to accusations of intellectual property theft, its net effect was a rise in the standards for inexpensive telecommunications equipment everywhere.[19]

In short, the value of coherence grows when a company expands across those geographic boundaries where its way to play and capabilities system are relevant. When considering new geographies, look for places where your distinctive capabilities can give you a right to win—and be skeptical about growth strategies that require an ever-expanding list of things you need to do well, just so you can compete everywhere. Being clear-minded about what your enterprise does well will be all the more important as markets continue to globalize and customers around the world have more access to information and goods from abroad. Seeking higher quality and lower costs, customers will gravitate toward products and services that provide better value, which inevitably means more attractiveness for companies with more coherence.

Emerging Markets

Sometimes people ask us if the need for coherence applies in emerging markets like Brazil, India, and China. These countries are typically hotbeds of entrepreneurialism, where startups must respond to opportunity rapidly and decisively. They seemingly can't slow down and focus on one capability system and way to play. These countries also tend to have highly active governments with idiosyncratic rules; success apparently depends less on business-related capabilities than on having good relationships with key officials and finding a protected niche in which to operate. As many outside companies entering emerging markets have discovered, it is very difficult to compete with either highly entrepreneurial locals or locals who enjoy government-sanctioned privileges. Why bother with coherence?

But this view is, in our opinion, misleading. A coherent capabilities system and way to play are more valuable in emerging markets than they might seem to be at first glance. The capabilities systems don't always look like those you would find in Europe or North America, but they can be just as focused, distinctive, and tied to a way to play. When the U.K. grocer Tesco entered Thailand, for example, it discovered that it could not easily supply fresh produce long-distance, as it did in its home country. Given the country's traffic congestion and poorly maintained roads, conventional refrigerated vehicles were impracticable. It was much more effective for Tesco to build another capability: sourcing fresh food from local growers, who existed near just about every store. This became a critical component of Tesco's strategy in Thailand and was so successful that Tesco became the largest food retail chain in the country. The strategy was later emulated in India by the large Indian retail chain Reliance.[20]

Many emerging-market enterprises compete by grounding their strategy in an in-depth understanding of the local market, that few outsiders (or insiders) can match. Their distinctive capabilities include not just dealing with regulation, but distribution, labor management, guerilla marketing, and inexpensive on-the-ground innovation. A good example is the China division of the global restaurant chain KFC (also known as Kentucky Fried Chicken, owned by Yum! Brands), which operates more or less as a self-contained business. As Edward Tse notes in *The China Strategy*, KFC is one of the most successful retail chains in China, even though it came from another continent with food, like fried chicken, that originally seemed alien to the Chinese culture. It took ten years for KFC to develop the capabilities it needed to be profitable in China, including the capability of finding and continually improving a menu adapted to Chinese taste, customs, and habits. Other critical capabilities included a dedicated logistics and distribution network—no easy task in China in the late 1990s. The restaurant also invested in ovens, so that KFC could offer more than fried food, and other technologies unique to the brand. Tse argues that it made a great difference that the company's China Division president Sam Su understood the Chinese culture and food business intimately. Even today, according to a manager who works for Su, "it takes five years for a local manager to develop an in-depth understanding of how to manage a Western-style fast-food restaurant."[21]

Many companies in emerging markets adopt a way to play as regulation navigators. They design their businesses to thrive by following (and influencing) governments rules and oversight, with capabilities to match. Regulation navigators exist all over the world, including in industrial economies, often in such sectors as health care and electric power. But it's important to remember that even the most monopolistic or regulated systems may eventually be deregulated. The forces of capitalism are simply very strong. When the moment of deregulation comes, the speed can be sudden and the dislocation can be severe; shares reallocate fast, and the better capabilities system will win at that time.

One company that discovered this firsthand was the Russian mobile telecommunications company VimpelCom, which competed for customers in 2003 after the privatization of the Russian telecom industry. Then-CEO Alexander Izosimov, looking back at this period, said that 80 percent of his company's market share was determined by its success during "hypergrowth," his name for this brief, frenetic, transition. "It's an experience that either kills your company or makes it stronger," he writes. During his company's first bout with hypergrowth in 2003 in Russia, "every meeting was a crisis meeting and every decision was made on panic mode."[22] Companies that have explicitly thought through a way to play and developed some of the entrepreneurial capabilities they will need will be far more advanced than competitors when this, or any other abrupt discontinuity, occurs.

Complex Conglomerates

Most large companies are already in several major businesses; some of these are multibillion-dollar businesses in their own right. Given this reality, must every company limit itself to one strategic trio—one way to play and one capabilities system, with all products and services matching? Haven't some conglomerates shown that they can operate with multiple strategies? GE, Textron, United Technologies Corporation, and Tata, for example, have built their strategic approaches on taking disparate businesses and knitting them together with their own versions of managerial glue: operational prowess, leadership development, effective allocation of capital, corporate culture, and the clout of their size and reputation. Aren't these businesses more effective together than they would be on their own?[23]

Perhaps. But in our view, the greatest value an enterprise can provide its parts is the delivery of a capabilities system. Being large, especially for the sake of scale, will in itself not add to that value, and will probably not win the day in the long term. The burden of proof is on the enterprise to show that being part of it adds more value than the incoherence penalty destroys. (The well-known conglomerate discount is the stock market's way of demanding the same proof.)

While many look at GE as proof that a diverse company can be successful, one great advantage for GE has been its relative coherence. When Jack Welch became CEO in 1981, he began honing down the company's portfolio from 150 businesses to 15.[24] GE's famous managerial initiatives, such as Workout and Six Sigma, spanned all of its businesses and provided the glue that other conglomerates lacked. Welch's name for this form of coherence was "integrated diversity."[25] It made GE a better competitor than most of the large companies that it went up against during that time; while most of those competitors had a narrower range of products and services, they were more incoherent.

In recent years, GE's industrial businesses, such as medical systems and industrial equipment, have done consistently better than its service businesses such as GE Capital, Kidder-Peabody, and NBC-TV. GE executive alumni have also tended to fare better in industrials and manufacturing than in financial services and retail companies. Could these be indicators that GE's coherence is grounded in capabilities like technological innovation and process improvement, which are more applicable to engineering-intensive businesses (like Honeywell, 3M, and Cooper Industries, successfully run by GE alumni) than to service businesses (like The Home Depot and Conseco, where GE alumni, taken on as CEOs, were ultimately forced to resign)?[26]

We suspect that it will get more and more difficult to maintain coherence across a range of businesses as broad as GE's. Moreover, the business world has moved on since Jack Welch's heyday, and if you are a leader in a large, multibusiness conglomerate, you undoubtedly face more coherent competition than you did in the past. If you are interested in raising an inquiry about your own coherence, there are two ways to start.

One starting point is within an individual business unit, where you can create a *pocket of coherence*: a self-contained operation with its own way to play, capabilities system, and lineup of products and services. Then begin to explore how the resulting coherence can spread, through functions and related product or service lines, to the rest of the enterprise. This strong starting point provides a platform for thinking about which parts of the business fit, which might be better off elsewhere, and why.

Alternatively, establish a top-down rationale for the structure of your corporation. Ask yourself: What are the sources of value that justify all of the businesses being part of the same corporation? They may already share services like human resources, finance, public relations, and regulatory compliance, and you may feel that these represent a form of glue. But are they the distinguishing capabilities that set your company apart from others? Do they reinforce one another, and are they aligned with a chosen way to play? Are they the system of capabilities that you would choose if you were starting from scratch, or are they simply the capabilities that are convenient to share right now? If the capabilities you share are not distinctive, then it may well be that the days of conglomerate benefit for your company, if they ever existed, are drawing to a close. A form of capabilities-driven strategy, in which different parts of your business become separate companies, each with a different way to play and capabilities system, may be the answer you are looking for.

The Path to Value

Given the complexities of incoherence and the choices necessary to move toward coherence, every company will find its own path. However, there are some universal principles to be aware of as you plot and take this journey.

The next chapter explains the basic process and stages of the capabilities-driven strategy. This is the path for increasing your coherence, becoming more coherent than your competitors, and gaining the corresponding value for your company.

CHAPTER THREE

THE CAPABILITIES-DRIVEN STRATEGY

Our description of coherence—having an aligned way to play, a capabilities system, and a lineup of products and services—is a final destination on a journey that could take years for most companies to achieve under normal business conditions. The capabilities-driven strategy provides a guide for accelerating your progress on this journey.

Like all broad initiatives, this process starts at the top, with the close involvement of the chief executive of the business (and, if applicable, the board). Because of the importance of execution, it will move into the rest of the organization as well. Each of the thousands of decisions made daily in your company can take you a little closer to coherence, or a little further away. Only by generating broad awareness of your way to play and engendering better use of your capabilities can you build an essential advantage for your company.

To accomplish this, you will be working across multiple dimensions of your complex organization at once. You'll look freshly at your situation and, in a strategic application of the scientific method, form and test hypotheses for your strategic direction before making a choice and committing your organization wholeheartedly to one of them. You'll develop strategies for growth, cost-cutting, and M&A—all reinforcing instead of contradicting each other. You'll move step by step, with each step increasing your ability to take the next. Within a few months, you'll do what only a few companies have managed to accomplish over the years: make a definitive choice about how you will deliver what your customers need, and in the process transform your company.

How a Company Reinvented Itself

In the mid-1990s, Johnson Controls, Inc. (JCI), an automobile components maker based in Milwaukee, conducted exactly this kind of exercise. JCI consisted of four principal businesses at the time. One made building controls such as thermostats (a device that the company's founder, Warren S. Johnson, had invented); another made plastic bottles; and a third made automotive batteries. The fourth, acquired in 1985, was Hoover Universal, a small company that made seats for motor vehicles. Renamed the Automotive Systems Group (ASG), it had enjoyed rapid growth under JCI; within ten years, it was making seats for eight million automobiles per year.

The existing way to play for this seat-components group was being a low-cost supplier (also known as a "value player"): snapping up market share by submitting the winning bids for seat programs designed by the major car manufacturers. JCI's added value in seats was the efficiency and speed of its manufacturing and delivery, which were exceptional; and it also had a relatively short-lived advantage in a labor pool that was lower-cost than that of the vehicle manufacturers. JCI was also one of the most advanced just-in-time suppliers, having developed the operational discipline to assemble and ship car and truck seats in sequence, so that the seats could be unloaded without sorting, to match them to the trim coats, colors, and other requirements of each car as it rolled along an assembly line.[1] This capability, among other things, had allowed JCI to acquire Toyota as a customer, which then enabled JCI to learn the world-class Toyota production system and develop its own prowess further.

But in 1994, the JCI management team looked more broadly at its business—and realized that the car-seat market was changing, creating new opportunities as well as imposing new forms of risk. Car makers in Detroit and Japan were starting to outsource more than just parts and components; they now increasingly looked to suppliers like JCI to provide full vehicle subsystems. Instead of delivering build-to-print specifications, an automaker would stipulate the weight, dimensions, and other criteria of a new vehicle platform and allow "Tier 1" suppliers like JCI to assume greater responsibility for the design of the seat systems and the performance of those designs.

This was such a different approach that JCI's car-seat business leaders set aside much of the next six months to discover its implications for their business. While the degree of de-integration varied by automaker and geography, the trend was clearly gaining momentum. Based on these shifting market dynamics, JCI's leaders identified four different ways to play in automotive seat systems. In order of increasing roles and responsibilities (and increasing levels of risk), they were:

- *Component supplier:* JCI could prototype and test the seats that car makers designed, using just-in-time, process control, and rapid-response capabilities to keep attracting customers.

- *Systems assembler:* JCI could deliver seats to detailed specs, producing and testing whole seat systems, building up its just-in-time and capacity planning capabilities, certifying suppliers, and developing a reputation for zero defects.

- *System integrator:* JCI could define the interfaces among seat components, integrate processes and designs with subsuppliers, develop new technologies, and build on its strategic sourcing and integrated delivery capabilities.

- *Solutions provider:* JCI could "design to concept": suggesting alternative designs based on market needs, proactively developing product innovations, and assuming the performance risks itself (by taking on product warranty liabilities).

Rather than leap to a choice, JCI's executives assessed these options and the capabilities required to succeed with each of them. Then they chose: They decided that they could add significant value by moving up the value chain to seat solutions provider, assuming higher levels of responsibility for end-user satisfaction and day-to-day problem-solving. This would be their optimal way to play. By getting involved earlier in the design process across multiple vehicle platforms, JCI could make good use of its expertise, economies of scale, and superior understanding of what automakers sometimes called "the golden butt": what consumers wanted most in a car seat.

Was being a solutions provider the only way to play in automotive seat systems? No. Indeed, JCI's primary competitors, Magna International and Lear, continued competing as system assemblers and integrators and remain in the business with those ways to play.

To be successful in its chosen way to play, JCI would have to build a system around a handful of mission-critical capabilities:

- *Customer management:* applying a consultative approach to selling valuable solutions, at the right prices

- *Early-stage engineering and design:* delivering technologically advanced products at low cost, and designing new innovations proactively, without waiting for guidance or specs from its customers

- *Shelf technology:* a critical capability that JCI hadn't developed before: reusing designs from one program to the next, thereby gaining scale and scope in product development

- *Integrated, just-in-time delivery:* optimizing JCI's existing lean manufacturing capabilities and network economics

- *Extended enterprise:* strategically exploiting vertical integration and maximizing the value of JCI's partnerships with its own smaller "Tier 2" subsuppliers

These capabilities were all important in isolation, but they became truly formidable as a group. To compete successfully as a solutions provider, JCI needed to excel in customer management and first-time engineering and design. To make a profit doing so, it needed to develop the strong shelf-technology capability, enabling it to reuse designs. To execute, it needed to sustain its existing leadership positions in

integrated just-in-time delivery and extended supplier relationships. Seeing how these were interconnected led to a moment of realization: JCI was better suited to car-seat design than any of its customers. GM, Chrysler, and Toyota had expertise only about their own seats. But the JCI engineers were specialists; they saw more seats than anyone else. If they kept developing and deploying their five capabilities together, they could gain a Michael Phelps–like advantage in the competitive arena.

The JCI team also knew the extent to which their company would have to transform itself to make this new strategy work. A year or two before, the company had opened a car-seat design and engineering center, with the idea of investing more heavily in innovation. That initiative had failed to yield profitable results, and in retrospect, one reason was clear: JCI had a long-standing tradition of de novo R&D; it created all-new seat designs from scratch for each new car platform. The cost would have been far less had ideas and technological solutions been applied from one car seat to the next. Now, engineers would finally have to give up their de novo approach.

The company would also have to decide which parts of the car seat to manufacture itself and which to outsource. For example, the senior team debated at length about the seat mechanism—the motor-and-switch combination that determines how a seat will move and tilt. Was it the specs (which JCI could hand off to a supplier) or the shaping of the metal and machine that differentiated the mechanism? In the end, the company decided to keep mechanisms in-house and continued refining them as part of its product portfolio.

When it came time to put its strategy into action, JCI followed through. Even though some of these decisions represented a break from its past, JCI's leaders maintained their commitment to being a whole-solutions provider, and the company evolved accordingly.

The results were outstanding in share price and profitability. JCI's market and management reputation soared, enabling the company to move from car seats to the design of auto interiors, a terrific move because it relied on the same capabilities system. To accomplish this, JCI purchased Prince, one of the most respected auto interior design firms, in 1996. Earnings growth over time was consistent and strong, and JCI successfully established an enduring essential advantage in the automotive interiors market.

A Process for Making Choices

JCI's story represents a good example of a capabilities-driven strategy. It shows how a challenge can lead to a new aspiration: aiming toward a new goal that represents a desired pathway forward, rather than simply a reaction or retrenchment. Because you can't design a way to play, a capabilities system, and a product and service portfolio in isolation, you must approach the journey to coherence as JCI did:

- You *discover* your choices. Through investigation and analysis, you come to a clearer understanding of your markets (including your customers and competition), your potential growth paths, and your capabilities. Rather than leap to a rapid decision, you develop hypotheses: credible options for a new way to play for your company.

- You *assess* each way to play in depth. Which hypotheses could give you the right to win in the market? And what would it take—in terms of capabilities —for each to succeed? What are the financial prospects, and the risks involved? One or more of these hypotheses will become the basis for the strategic direction of your organization.

- You *choose* a direction, a single way to play, and one capabilities system as the basis of your ongoing strategy. This is a significant exercise for the executive team and the major stakeholders of the organization and often includes the board. In choosing this direction, you set in motion a new way of doing business; you must therefore commit to it wholeheartedly.

- You set out to *transform* the company. You engage the rest of the company's leaders in tough decisions about where to channel your next wave of investment. You design and communicate the implementation steps and portfolio moves needed to build or deploy the necessary capabilities and to reinforce and execute the new direction of the business. You take your first actions toward coherence, divesting parts of the business and reshaping others, sparking "moments of truth" that raise general awareness of the changes that are coming.

- You enable your company to *evolve* into the kind of organization that can stay coherent over time. You continue to engage the commitment of people at every level and develop the practices and relationships that will foster this strategy on the ground.

Figure 3-1 shows the overall process in schematic form. Though the details can vary from one company to the next, there are always several critical features. In the first three stages, you make a choice: Discovery leads to several hypotheses about your way to play, which you then assess and narrow down, preparing for the moment, when, like the JCI leaders, you define your distinctive potential. Then, in the last two stages, you enable the choice (transformation) and live the choice (evolution).

You can see that the process involves intensive give-and-take between different groups—a core team of carefully selected project leaders, the top team of senior management, and the rest of the staff throughout the enterprise. We'll discuss this process and its stages in more detail in chapter 10.

This process can occur at the level of a significant business (like JCI's seats business); it can also take place at the enterprise level of a larger, multibusiness company. In either case, the basic sequence is roughly the same (although, as we'll see in chapter 10, there are some special considerations for the enterprise level).

Overcoming the Incentives for Incoherence

Once you make a choice and commit to it, you will set in motion a movement toward coherence, raising your most effective businesses, brands, and services in importance. There may be painful outcomes as well. For instance, the four big initiatives you had slated for next year may no longer make sense, given the capabilities you are now focused on. You may need to step in to halt them, along with other investments that are under way.

The tendency to relapse will be strong, and it's important to understand where the incentives for incoherence come from. Some of them have to do with your history. Most companies of any size are complex. They evolved in messy and incoherent ways, dealing with ever-changing

FIGURE 3-1

Overview of a capabilities-driven strategy

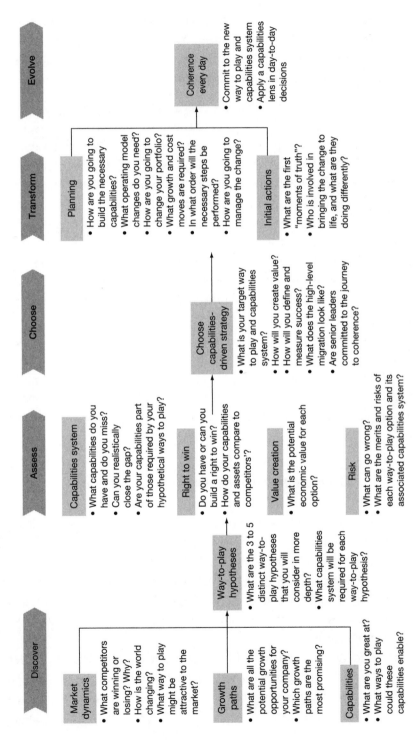

Source: Booz & Company.

and inconsistent business environments as well as their own internal idiosyncrasies. The legacy of that evolution is a host of programs, processes, and imperatives, each with its own constituents. Many people have come to think of these incoherent practices as simply, "the way we do things around here," a habit that has become etched into their neural pathways.[2]

Efforts to improve customer insight, for example, seem natural and laudatory—but they can lead a business unit leader at your company to propose bringing out a product line extension ("Consumers are asking for it") without considering how it fits with your capabilities system. A benchmarking exercise might lead a functional leader to argue for new investment in distribution networks, because "our competitors have them" or "we must be great at this"—without recognizing that your existing distribution network, while it may not be the best, is more than adequate for your way to play, and the investment is better made elsewhere. Fear of getting left behind might lead another executive to say, "Our customers are going to digital media, and we have to figure out the new marketing model," in a business where digital media is not a primary driver of demand. The need to size the potential customer base for a new offering might result in optimistic estimates that aren't really applicable, because your company's way to play will not succeed in that market.

Some incentives of incoherence—or, more accurately, disincentives to fight incoherence—can come directly from external stakeholders: regulators, suppliers, customers, and particularly Wall Street. To be sure, in the long run, capital markets channel their investment to more coherent companies. But in the short run, companies can often get higher valuations by making incoherent moves, like across-the-board cost cuts, that temporarily boost earnings. If you have been playing that game, your stock price may improve in the short term, only to decline over time. Conversely, outside stakeholders may object if you decide to divest some businesses that are highly profitable, but that do not fit your way to play or use the same capabilities. These stakeholders may not recognize the way they are distracting the rest of your business.

You may be tempted itself by opportunities that—while they don't fit your capabilities system or way to play—seem like "sure bet" or "must-do" options for expanding into new geographies, products, or services. Some of these unnecessary activities might represent a hedge against the possibility that other things you try will fail. During good economic times, you may underestimate the risks of incoherence in these growth moves, because you don't feel the penalty; its effects are masked by the general upswing.

These types of moves feel right, in part, because they historically conferred advantage. The first company to offer a new product or gain a particular asset had transient, first-mover advantage. The company with the greatest market share had economies of scale; indeed, this became part of the justification for growth, as companies vied to take advantage of scale in their back-office operations, customer reach efforts, and distribution channels. Similarly, the company that paid the closest attention to its customers, through methods such as market research and segmentation, could best offer them what they were looking for.

But the advantages of scale, and even of first-mover advantage, have diminished in recent years. Technology, cheap information, and outsourcing have conspired to lower the barriers to entry once erected and maintained by scale, and to dramatically reduce the minimum efficient scale point in many manufacturing businesses. Market-back approaches to strategy are today insufficient for success in most established industries. This doesn't mean that companies should disregard market signals; all strategy is set within that all-important context. But companies should consider both external market prospects *and* the internal capabilities system required to exploit these prospects successfully and sustainably. The focal point of your strategy should be where these two perspectives intersect.

As you take the journey to coherence, you and your company will move away from all of these incoherent habits and toward full commitment to success in the activities that matter. Since some people—inside and outside your company—won't intuitively recognize the logic of your strategy, you will have to clarify it for them. They may include the board and executive team, along with your employees, investors, customers, and suppliers. Learn to communicate your way to play and its rationale clearly and consistently, time and again, in the same language. Bring others in your company to a point where they can do the same.

Make the most of the coherence you already have. Every company we've ever seen has had pockets of coherence that can be exploited from day one. Procter & Gamble and 3M invested heavily in corporate R&D during the 2000s, precisely for this reason: each company's innovation capability was already highly valued, but not widely deployed enough. By publicizing it (for example, with P&G's Connect and Deliver program), they encouraged people within the company to think about applying their innovation systems to a broader range of products and services.

Use every growth program, cost-reduction effort, or functional strategy as an opportunity to reinforce your way to play. Set a policy, for example, that your company will only benchmark distinctive capabilities, relevant to your way to play—regardless of which industry you find them in. Think in terms of coherence every time you outsource: is it a distinctive capability that you should keep in-house or a capability that you can buy? Judge shared services the same way. Which functions are linked to distinctive capabilities and thus deserve the most investment? When you promote or transfer people, among other factors, consider the impact this will have on critical capabilities.

Find ways to recognize and unravel the incentives and habitual operations that steer your company toward incoherence. For example, empower your functional leaders to give priority to requests that are tied to the chosen way to play and capabilities system. Guard against the natural human tendency to label *everything* as connected to your way to play and capabilities system, so that it gets support or avoids the cost-cutting ax.

In Chapter 12, we'll look more closely at your role as the leader. For now, it's enough to remind yourself of Mahatma Gandhi's famous quote: "We need to be the change we wish to see in the world."[3] If you are leading this effort, people will look to you to be an example of coherence. That will be your responsibility—and, you may find, it will also be your pleasure.

Getting Started

To begin with, complete a coherence test of your company (table 3-1) — a diagnostic assessment of the coherence that currently exists in the thinking and actions of your senior leadership. This diagnostic exercise will challenge your perceptions and those of your colleagues. You may

TABLE 3-1

The coherence test

In a small group, talk through the answers to these questions as candidly as possible. This exercise benefits from more than one person's perspective. The two columns of questions reflect that incoherence has two sources—strategic and operational. The more questions to which you can truthfully answer "yes," the more coherent your company.

Can we state it?	Do we live it?
Way to play	
Are we clear about how we choose to create value in the marketplace?	Are we investing in the capabilities that really matter to our way to play?
Capabilities system	
Can we articulate the three to six capabilities that describe what we do uniquely better than anyone else?	Do all our businesses draw on this superior capabilities system?
Have we defined how they work together in a system?	Do our organizational structure and operating model support and leverage it?
Do our strategy documents reflect this?	Does our performance management system reinforce it?
Product and service fit	
Have we specified our product and service "sweet spot"?	Do most of the products and services we sell fit with our capabilities system?
Do we understand how to leverage the capabilities system in new or unexpected arenas?	Are new products and acquisitions evaluated on the basis of their fit with the way to play and capabilities system?
Coherence	
Can everyone in the organization articulate our differentiating capabilities?	Do we have a right to win in our chosen market?
Is our company's leadership reinforcing these capabilities?	Do all of our decisions add to our coherence, or do some of them push us toward incoherence?

Source: Adapted from Paul Leinwand and Cesare Mainardi, "The Coherence Premium," *Harvard Business Review*, June 2010, 86–92.

be surprised by how your existing perceptions of your supposedly best products and services, your highest-growth markets, or your most significant competitors differ.

This exercise will give you a more complete understanding of where you stand; keep it at the back of your mind as you read through the next six chapters, as we'll revisit it in chapter 10. Use this diagnostic more than once—it's a valuable tool to measure and track your company's progress on your journey to coherence.

For an online version of the coherence test, visit
www.theessentialadvantage.com.

It's difficult for individuals to objectively take stock of their capabilities—to assess what they're good at and what they're not—and it's even more difficult for companies. Try to look as dispassionately at your company as a knowledgeable investor would. Be prepared for the coherence test to show that your senior team is not as aligned as you expected. We sometimes ask corporate leaders, "If we were to interview everybody in your management team and ask them to identify the capabilities that are most critical to the advantage in your business, would they describe the same three to six things?" There is always a moment's pause—and then a recognition that the leaders are not as aligned as they would like to be. But there is also generally a recognition of the chance to focus, to eliminate distraction, and to move past consensus to a new type of choice.

Discovering the Elements

In the rest of this book, you will read about the choices needed to develop your own strategic elements: how your way to play, your capabilities system, and your lineup of products and services can all fit together. It is tempting to think of these as three separate elements, conceived individually. One could imagine selecting a way to play in light of your perception of your market, figuring out a capabilities system close to the one you already have, and then deciding which products and services to keep or sell.

But, as we've seen in this chapter, a capabilities-driven strategy doesn't work that way. So as you read the next three chapters, imagine yourself entering your own discovery phase for each of these elements: chapter 4 on the way to play, chapter 5 on the capabilities system, and chapter 6 on the fit of products and services. Then in chapters 7 through 9, you'll learn how a capabilities-driven strategy can drive value in your company. In chapters 10 through 12, you will learn how to lay the groundwork for the rest of your journey and how to live coherence in your company every day.

II

ELEMENTS OF A CAPABILITIES-DRIVEN STRATEGY

CHAPTER FOUR

THE WAY TO PLAY

Since 1990, the largest retail chain in the world has been Walmart.[1] It has more than 3,500 stores, more than three hundred product categories on its shelves, more than two million employees, and about one-third of the U.S. population visiting its stores each week. Dozens of books have been published about the chain, recounting the unique value proposition set forth by its founder, Sam Walton ("Save money, live better") and its growth from a small-town Arkansas merchandiser to its immense scale and scope.

Most observers attribute the chain's success to its impressive logistics operations, its ability to get vendors to fall in line, or its position as a low-cost retailer. But having one or two superior capabilities or a compelling strategy in itself is not enough. Many retailers have tried to market themselves to cost-conscious customers, with far more limited results. What really underlies Walmart's competitive advantage is a coherent system that involves its strategy, capabilities, and offerings and that lowers the company's total value-chain cost in a differentiated manner.

It starts with a precise and powerful way to play. Walmart is a big-box provider of everything from groceries to electronics to houseplants at "always low prices," largely without special sales or discounts. It has, more or less without exception, stuck to this strategic approach since its founding in 1962. Its preferred customers have always been the same: price-sensitive shoppers and "brand aspirationals" (highly cost-conscious consumers who seek out brand-name products). You won't find a Walmart store on Fifth Avenue in New York, the Champs-Elysées in Paris, or alongside Nordstrom, Saks Fifth Avenue, or Neiman-Marcus in an upscale shopping mall. That would not be consistent with Walmart's chosen way of creating value in the market.

Over the years, Walmart has built and carefully honed a remarkable capabilities system to enable and support that way to play. First, it wrings maximum efficiency from its supply chain, integrating aggressive vendor management techniques, expert point-of-sale data analytics (its famous retail-link system), superior logistics, and rigorous working-capital management. Another capability is the unparalleled mastery of "location, location, location": the selection and acquisition of real estate, especially in rural and suburban North America. Finally, Walmart has a sophisticated capability embedded in its retail conception and design, which it uses to craft an ambience of wholesome, no-frills friendliness (like that of Southwest Airlines) that makes its preferred customers feel welcome. These three capabilities work together to enable Walmart to outpace other retailers in getting the right product to the right store in the right quantity with remarkable efficiency.

Everything Walmart does is thus matched tightly to its preferred customers and hence to its way to play. The retailer does not sell big-ticket items like furniture or large appliances, where it could not have a meaningful cost advantage. Nor does it sell items such as music CDs with explicit lyrics that run counter to its customers' values. It innovates constantly within its chosen constraints: opening mini-clinics in its stores or tailoring its product assortments to local consumption trends. Walmart product buyers can identify hundreds of traits to define the assortment for any given store; a sporting goods buyer, for example, might use "freshwater" to designate a Minneapolis store and "saltwater" for a store in Plymouth, Massachusetts. Walmart's capabilities also allow it to feed vendors better information than they have themselves about customers; this increases the company's leverage with suppliers and allows it to move inventory with extraordinary efficiency. Finally, while reaching out for new customers, Walmart also finds ingenious avenues for growth within its existing customer base and its ongoing way to play. (In chapter 7, we'll describe Walmart's renewed growth strategy in more detail.)[2]

Walmart's most visible U.S. competitor, Target Stores, might seem at first glance to be aiming at the same general market segment, but Target has a different way to play. Target—often pronounced with a mock-French accent ("Tar-zhay") by devotees—similarly seeks to save its customers money. But it also provides fashion-forward merchandise for image-conscious consumers. Everything from the store layout to its advertising to its inventory is intended to convey an eye for style. For example, the lack of piped music and the minimal use of public address announcements makes the store feel clean, spare, and frugally upscale.

Target's way to play was developed through a thirty-year evolution within the Dayton Hudson department store chain (formerly known for its flagship Marshall Fields), which changed its name to the Target Corporation in 2000 and closed or sold its other brands soon thereafter. The capabilities system that supports this way to play includes image advertising, the management of urban locations (which Walmart generally does not have), and a distinctive approach to "mass prestige" sourcing, including the cultivation of exclusive partnerships with some of the world's leading designers, such as Mossimo Giannulli and Michael Graves. To match the needs of its younger, more urban customer base, it sells furniture and more clothing than Walmart.

Another of Target's important capabilities involves pricing. Target carefully monitors prices to ensure that on selected high-profile items, the kind that draw people into the store, it matches the prices of Walmart and other competitors. But in its other merchandise, Target moves "up the pricing ladder" more rapidly than Walmart, carrying an assortment of higher-priced, higher-value items that appeal to more affluent, fashion-conscious shoppers (and that provide the retailer with larger margins).[3]

Now consider Kmart, the last and least successful member of the U.S. big-discounter triad (coincidentally, all three retail chains launched operations in 1962). In and out of bankruptcy in the early 2000s, Kmart is still struggling to define its way to play in the mass-market retail space. It describes itself on its corporate Web site as a "mass merchandising company that offers customers quality products through a portfolio of exclusive brands and labels."[4] That could describe any retailer from Old Navy to The Home Depot.

As a Walmart customer, you know you'll save money and still feel welcome. At Target, you know you'll get fashionable products at prices that feel reasonable. What, then, is Kmart's niche? Walk though a store, and you'll discover designers like Martha Stewart and Jaclyn Smith in the low-budget ambience of a warehouse. Since its merger with Sears, Roebuck and Co. in 2005, Kmart has started carrying Kenmore appliances in its stores. This is a high-potential growth move, given the strength of the Kenmore brand, but it may require the high-touch expert sales assistance that many Sears customers expect.

In short, Kmart has not established an identifiable way to play—a way that reflects both its customers' needs and its own capabilities. Harry Cunningham, the founder of Kmart, reportedly admitted that Sam Walton "not only copied our concepts, he strengthened them."[5] This lack of a clear concept about how to reach the market is probably the single most important factor in explaining why Kmart's fortunes have fallen so far, compared with its two rivals.

Aspiration, Reality, and Choice

Every consistently successful company that we know has a clear understanding of what differentiates it as an enterprise: specifically, the way it creates value for the people who buy its products and services. This is their way to play in the market. A well-developed way to play is a chosen position in the market, grounded in a view of your own capabilities and where the market is going. It represents what Gary Hamel and C. K. Prahalad called "strategic intent": a sense of direction that can prompt a group of people to stretch beyond their day-to-day goals or, as the authors put it, "the dream that energizes a company."[6] A way to play is both realistic and aspirational. It recognizes the achievements and limits of the past, is oriented toward what you hope and expect to do in the future, and gives you a clear rationale for the choices you will make between now and then.

Developing a way to play is not a casual undertaking or an academic exercise. It is the pivotal moment in a capabilities-driven strategy (as described in chapter 10). You will live by this choice and develop it for years, and maybe forever. A way to play is both "capabilities-forward" and "market-back"; to develop it, you look outward, with acute analysis and observation of your industry (and how it is changing), your customers, and your competition. You also look inward, at the capabilities you can build and the limits on that potential; you should not take on a way to play that you can't possibly master. Above all, you identify and codify what is distinctive about you now, and how you hope to be distinctive in the future. In most cases, you are far better off understanding what you do well and looking for the markets that will respond than you are looking for attractive markets and trying to design a way to play to reach them, no matter what it may take to deliver.

We are sometimes asked if there is a danger of a company's picking the wrong way to play—a strategy that is not right for its market. Certainly, it's possible, but a much more common problem is not to pick a way to play at all. Many companies just respond opportunistically to what they think their various customers demand. They then keep shifting as demands change: lowering prices, making heroic efforts to meet a short-term need, or expanding to new "adjacent" segments. Other companies maintain a complex array of products and services that makes seeing through to any one way to play impossible. This does not create value; such companies tend to eke out growth and profit numbers by endless cost cuts and typically cannot sustain performance, particularly when a more coherent competitor appears.

If your process for defining a way to play is rigorous enough and you know your business sufficiently well, you are likely to see a way to create value. Your ability to capture that value depends on whether you can act sooner, faster, and more effectively than your competition. The goal of a capabilities-driven strategy is to help you hone your judgment about your way to play, to make a choice, and to put it into action.

Puretone Ways to Play

You can generally start thinking about your company's way to play by looking at common, generic ways of creating value. These are what we call *puretone* ways to play. They may not fully capture your business. But when you mix a few puretone ways to play in a well-defined way, like mixing primary colors, you might end up with a more precise hue that reflects your company's best strategy. In some sectors, you might stay fairly close to a puretone; for example, you could be a value player. But in most cases, you will end up crafting your own distinctive way to play, with puretones as a starting point.

Table 4-1 shows the puretones we work with most frequently. Most of them are commonly observed in the business literature; for example, at least six major books have been published on the "experience provider" way to play.[7] This list is illustrated with business examples that are evocative but not always a complete description of the company. For instance, McDonald's is a longstanding experience provider—as well as a textbook example of a value player. So we included it as an example of both puretones.

For worksheets and exercises on your own puretones, visit
www.theessentialadvantage.com.

In real life, very few companies have only one puretone way to play. Most successful ways to play are combinations or refinements of several puretones, although sometimes they have a major "hue." For example, IKEA, the global leader in home furnishings design and retail, is primarily a value player; its way to play is evident in its slogan: "affordable solutions for better living." But this Swedish company, which designs and sells its wares for a broad global consumer market, has also established itself as an innovator (for example, it designs its own furniture and creates its own distinctive paints, lacquers, and finishes), and, to some extent, as an experience provider—its distinctive store layout, play areas with free pagers for parents, and Swedish-style in-store restaurants make people want to spend time in its stores.

Looking at puretones can help you see the differentiation in an industry. In many sectors, corporate ways to play have shaped the market as they evolved, allowing two or more players in the industry to sustain profitable businesses in very different ways. Consider, for example, the personal computer manufacturing industry—where companies have carved out identities according to different combinations of puretones.

Acer: Founded in Taiwan in 1973, Acer is a value player, but it has resisted commoditization by also being a fast follower and a

TABLE 4-1

Puretone ways to play

Puretone way to play	Value proposition	Business example	Comments
Aggregator	Provides the convenience of a one-stop solution	eBay Granger	These companies pull together multiple suppliers or sources under one common experience.
Category leader	Maintains top market share in a category and uses that position to shape and influence downstream channels as well as upstream supply markets	Coca-Cola Philip Morris Intel L'Oréal GE	These companies often develop mass marketing capabilities that provide broad market appeal, combined with a high level of influence on both the value chain and the retail channels of the entire category.
Consolidator	Dominates an industry through acquisitions ("rolling up an industry") to provide either a value benefit to consumers or access to a platform with products and services that otherwise would not be possible	Cisco Systems Microsoft	Consolidators acquire rivals and offer customers access, technology, or prices that no smaller or less comprehensive company can provide.
Customizer	Leverages insight and market intelligence to offer tailored products or services	Dell Burger King	The Internet, with its interoperability, automation of customer insight, global reach, and lowered transaction costs, has made it easier to succeed as a customizer.
Disintermediator	Helps customers bypass unreachable or more expensive distribution channels and parts of the value chain, thereby providing access to otherwise inaccessible services and products	NAPA Auto Parts Priceline 3PLs (third-party logistics firms)	To deliver its way to play, a disintermediator must provide enhanced value for its customers, usually by cutting costs or aggregating volume. For example, the 3PLs provide "on-demand transportation"—in consumer packaged

(continued)

TABLE 4-1 (*continued*)

Puretone way to play	Value proposition	Business example	Comments
			goods, these firms can take over an entire distribution chain, with capabilities they deploy on behalf of all their clients.
Experience provider	Builds enjoyment, engagement, and emotional attach-ment through strong brands or experiences	McDonald's Starbucks Apple Virgin Airlines and other Virgin companies Some hotel chains Luxury and sports car makers	Unlike premium play-ers, these businesses can be viable at all price segments. In many U.S. communities, for the price of a Happy Meal, McDonald's provides the most accessible and engaging indoor playground available. Experience providers can also include those manufacturers who make the use or purchase of their product feel like a noteworthy event.
Fast follower	Leverages founda-tions laid by innova-tors to quickly introduce competing offerings, often at greater value or to a broader base of consumers	Hyundai Wrigley (see chapter 6) Chinese *shan zhai* companies	Many successful innovations (e.g., the steamboat, electric power, television, personal computer) were spread through fast followers that successfully marketed someone else's innovation.
Innovator	Introduces new and creative products or services to the market	Apple Procter & Gamble 3M Honeywell Nokia Philips	These are not just introducers of new products or services, but companies whose ongoing innovative capability enables them to consistently win and hold cus-tomers. There are many types of innovators, and the most successful ways to play clearly define the type of innovation and why it distin-guishes a particular company.

Puretone way to play	Value proposition	Business example	Comments
Platform provider	Operates and oversees a shared resource or infrastructure	Electric power utilities New York Stock Exchange FedEx Cognizant Conrail Back-office trans-action processors Natural resource providers (oil, natural gas, forest prod-ucts, and mining companies)	These companies create a platform or resource that others can share by doing business with them. Whether they are heavily regulated or not, they have an implicit role as stewards of the resource they manage.
Premium player	Offers high-end products or services	Herman Miller BMW Nordstrom Most luxury goods companies	Customers pay for both status and perceived value: customer service (Nordstrom), artistry (Herman Miller), performance (BMW).
Regulation navigator	Offers access to otherwise unreach-able products and services by managing within government rules and oversight, and by influencing them	Health insurance companies China National Off-Shore Oil Corporation Industrial and Commercial Bank of China Some trading companies (Mitsui)	These companies are viable in nations and sectors where govern-ments control or regu-late a large percentage of business activity. The CEO of a Turkish company once remarked that in a pre-deregulation environment, it was important to operate in many product lines, to have allies in multiple ministries, because pleasing the government was more important than pleas-ing customers. These companies can be vulnerable if regulation frameworks change.
Reputation player	As a trustworthy provider, charges a premium or gains privileged access to customers	Tata Seventh Generation Volvo	The reputational attribute is not neces-sarily altruistic, but it is tied to a value other than saving money. Volvo's reputation for

(continued)

TABLE 4-1 (*continued*)

Puretone way to play	Value proposition	Business example	Comments
		Whole Foods Toyota, BP, and Goldman Sachs (before their troubles in 2010)	safety was arguably a compelling factor in its 2010 purchase by the Chinese company Geely Motors. This way to play can backfire if a company lacks the capabilities or attention to follow through and its reputation erodes (Enron was a failed reputation player), and it often depends on close connection with a dedicated, affiliated group of customers.
Risk absorber	Mitigates or pools market risk for its customers	Commodity hedge funds Many insurance companies	Risk absorbers enable others to extend entrepreneurially or help them navigate uncertainty.
Solutions provider	Provides bundled products and services that fully address customer needs	Ahlstrom Johnson Controls, Inc. IBM Lockheed Martin	This group is also known as integrators, because the way to play depends on the capability to fit together disparate technologies and practices, including those from customers.
Value player	Offers lowest prices or tremendous value for comparable products and services	Walmart Southwest Airlines, JetBlue, Ryanair Tata Motors (with the Nano) McDonald's IKEA	Also known as low-cost producers, successful value players have the capabilities to sustain their position without falling into a commoditization spiral of price-based competition.

consolidator. Over the years, Acer has bought dozens of computer businesses, including Gateway, Packard-Bell, and the personal computer division of Texas Instruments. Acer is also a particular type of aggregator, acting as a gatekeeper to Asian innovation and low-cost manufacturing, packaging the "Wild East" technology in more accessible form. The company buys massive quantities of parts—such as processors, hard drives, and video cards—and assembles them into personal computers that can't be beat on price. To match consumer needs, Acer depends on insight from big-box retailers about what consumers will pay for different configurations.

Apple: This company's way to play combines being an innovator, an experience provider, and a premium player. Apple makes devices that intuitively fit with the way people work, play, and learn, and it provides the complexity of a full-featured computer or media environment with the simplicity of an appliance and a high level of technological control. Apple's way to play dates back to the early 1980s, when the company pioneered the first commercialized graphical user interface. It famously bears the mark of longtime CEO Steve Jobs, who leads the company as an impresario might lead a theatrical group. The same way to play applies in all the sectors where the company does business—hardware, software, telephones, portable devices, the online iTunes service, and the Apple retail stores—which few observers thought would succeed when the first one opened in McLean, Virginia, in 2001.[8] Some capabilities, such as manufacturing, are table stakes; these are consequently deemphasized and outsourced. The difficulty and distinction of Apple's way to play is obvious: no other company has chosen it. For years, the company was considered marginal in the personal computer industry, with a relatively small market share; only in the 2000s did it gain enterprise value commensurate with its influence on innovation.

Dell: This consummate customizer, value player, and aggregator has been positioned for years as the leader of the direct-sales model, which distinguishes it from Acer and other value players like Lenovo. Dell offers computers with leading-edge technology—assembled from a broad group of suppliers, sold directly over the Web or the phone, tailored to individual needs, and made available quickly and reliably. This traditionally gave Dell a 15 percent cost advantage: because customers paid only for the components they wanted and avoided the expenses of computer stores, they paid a lower price than did purchasers of prebuilt systems. In 2007, as the company navigated some product quality and service challenges, Michael Dell returned as CEO. Dell now faces the challenge that, as hardware costs have fallen, the value of customization may not be as significant.

Hewlett-Packard: Once known as an innovator, Hewlett-Packard has developed a way to play that is closer to a consolidator and a solutions provider. It spent $25 billion on acquisitions between 2000 and 2010, buying Compaq, Electronic Data Systems Corporation (EDS), Mercury Interactive, 3Com (known for inventing the Internet protocol), Palm Computing, and many smaller software companies. In recent years, HP has pulled these together with its own engineers to provide end-to-end, Web-based computer services for businesses and individual customers. The company draws on open systems and platforms, delivering a high level of convenience and accessibility—starting with a Web site that features courses and services like Web site design as prominently as it features laptops and printers. HP competes increasingly with other large systems providers, such as Cisco and IBM. Its printers, calculators, and other devices continue to sell, but they are increasingly marketed as part of an integrated system in which customers, as well as employees, sign up for the famous "HP Way" and expect to be taken care of.

Although to a casual observer these manufacturers may seem to compete against one another, they have carved out very different approaches to the personal computer market, and they attract different customers accordingly. Their ways to play are distinctive, highly relevant to particular groups of customers, and closely tied to their company's roots. Apple has a renowned and distinctive approach to design, but it could not do what Acer, with its roots near low-cost China, does. HP's heritage in instruments and integration has similarly given it an edge in delivering innovative services (no matter whether it developed or acquired them). Dell's origins in founder Michael Dell's dormitory room, where he built computers to order for customers, led directly to its advanced supply-chain management and customization capabilities.

Now imagine starting a personal computer business. Your first strategic priority would be to find a way to play that was not covered by the companies described here. Similarly, if you were to open a new retail chain in the United States, you would look for a distinctive way to play and a corresponding capabilities system, neither of which could overlap those of Walmart or Target. You would probably not try to beat the computer makers or the retailers at their own games (unless you saw a weakness in their capabilities systems). Your success would depend on finding a game that you could play better than anybody else.

Building a Better Way to Play

How, then, do you get from a list of puretones to a way to play that will carry your company forward? In forming hypotheses and conducting in-depth reviews and workshops, you are looking for the critical insight: the spark of recognition that represents your company's particular contribution to value.

We've already described that spark of recognition at Pfizer Consumer Healthcare (claims-based marketing, in chapter 1) and JCI (becoming the most expert designer and manufacturer of auto seats, in chapter 3). A more recent case occurred in 2010, when the executive team of a large food manufacturer decided to seek its own sweet spot. The executives saw an opportunity to build a major new business in prepackaged convenience food, and they started with three puretones that summed up three ways to do it:

Category leader: The company would become the most visible brand for its leading products, shaping the most important categories by increasing market share. To accomplish this, it would focus resources where it truly understood customer needs, and where it could build a better value proposition than its competitors.

Innovator: The company would rapidly develop and launch new types of packaged foods, taking into account trends and customer interest, and thus become the company known for leading-edge nutrition and convenience.

Solutions provider: It would give people "the meals they asked for": providing prepared foods that could be easily combined by busy working families into customized ready-to-serve meals, while visibly seeking out consumer requests for healthier foods and responding with new offerings.

As they explored the external market in depth, the executives realized that there was an attractive market for each of these approaches—large and incompletely served by the current food industry. If they took on any of the three, they could profitably gain market share and solidify their brand identity in unprecedented ways. All three had roughly the same potential for increasing enterprise value. But the lightbulbs went on for the executive team only when the functional leaders began talking about the capabilities each approach would require.

"These are three different sets of investments," said the manufacturing leader, "and we can't do them all." He went on to explain the differences in supply-chain management for each way to play. As a category leader, the company would need to cut costs and seek economies of scale while raising its manufacturing prowess: investing in process technologies and executional effectiveness. Becoming an innovator would mean configuring a flexible value chain that could launch new products rapidly and economically. The solutions-provider approach would mean a different type of flexibility: providing more packaged food sold at different temperatures—some frozen, some fresh. It would also mean building a more direct, collaborative relationship between operations and R&D.

The head of marketing and sales said she could see similar differences: "The merchandising forces would have almost no overlap." As a category leader, the company would seek to own the shelf (or the sector) through sharp-pencil tactics (tightly tailored to each brand and local region) for pricing, promotion, and merchandising. The innovator way to play would emphasize another type of advertising and promotion: communicating the new consumer value propositions while ensuring rapid, widespread retail distribution of new products. Being a solutions provider would move the company directly into engagement with consumers, through online Web sites and other social media, displays for the store perimeters, and a great deal of marketing experimentation.

Suddenly, this was no longer a conversation about the market and its demands. It was a conversation about the company's own capabilities and how the executive team might marshal those capabilities together. Where did the company really have strengths? Which trade-offs were the team members willing to make? Around they went, working through the discovery and assessment stages of the capabilities-driven strategy that we described in chapter 3, focusing their attention not just on the capabilities they had, but on those they were willing and able to build. Originally, they had expected to adopt the innovator way to play because it meant a higher-margin business. But after several meetings spread over the course of three weeks, they decided they had a better chance of gaining the expected amount of enterprise value as the category leader, because that fit the capabilities system that they already had. This decision has, so far, begun to pay off for them.

These types of insights don't stem from a recipe book; there is no analytical formula for reaching them. But by starting with puretones and looking at their ramifications, you can draw on your team's business acumen without being held back by old preconceptions. Just as Apple is not a pure innovator, HP is not a pure consolidator, and IKEA is not a pure value player, you must refine these puretones into more precise articulations of your company's potential future.

Criteria for Judging Effectiveness

If your way to play successfully addresses the market, the potential for differentiation, the dynamics of your industry, and the feasibility of the approach, then it has a very good chance of success. Evaluate your proposed strategy using this checklist.

There is a market that will value your way to play

In other words, there is a sufficient number of chosen customers who will find your way to play meaningful. In determining the potential value in a market, we (like Michael Porter, Ted Levitt, and many others) recommend looking at the needs of customers, not at the way your production category is conventionally defined. Pay attention to "substitutes":

unexpected products that perform similar functions in different ways.[9] If you produce customer-relationship management software and sales have dropped off, chances are your customers are spending not on a rival software package, but on Internet-based "cloud computing" services and analytics. If you make frozen foods, and a father isn't buying your dinosaur-shaped chicken nuggets in the frozen-foods aisle, he may be buying the (nonfrozen) Organic Meals for Tots or taking his kids to a restaurant. If you're a steel supplier, and a vehicle maker switches from you to another source, it may be to composites (engineered materials such as fiberglass or carbon fiber). A high number of substitutes in any sector may indicate that you haven't yet found the right way to play or that you have more room for growth. In table 10-1 (chapter 10), we show a variety of tests for assessing the potential markets for your way to play.

Your way to play is differentiated from your competitors' ways to play

In chapter 10, we'll look more closely at ways to analyze yourself and your competitors to see whether your way to play (along with your capabilities system and lineup of products and services) gives you the right to win. For the moment, it is enough to recognize the way in which your proposed way to play would compete with others. Having the same way to play as your competitors can work out advantageously if you have a better capabilities system, but in many cases it's better to differentiate. Like the computer companies described earlier in this chapter, have you developed a distinct way to play that your competitors can't emulate?

Your way to play will be relevant, given the changes that might take place in your industry

If you're in a rapidly evolving industry, then your way to play should be tested against the external changes you see ahead. They don't have to be certain, but if they are plausible and would affect your business, you need to take them into account. To test your way to play in light of external changes, engage in deliberate conversation about the dangers and risks of the changing industry, as well as the opportunities, and how you would respond. To be sure, as Clayton Christensen has pointed out, the ingrained capabilities that made you effective in the past—especially those that support your existing way to play—can make it difficult to change in the future.[10] But the more clearly you understand how you add value, the more likely you are to see a discontinuity coming—and to be able to adapt to it effectively.

Some companies have deliberately tried to cultivate their ability to see discontinuities—so that, when their industry is ready to change, they have the time and awareness they need to look for growth outside their existing businesses. For these companies, paying attention to potential discontinuities is not a one-time event, but an endeavor that requires sustained organizational focus. In 2007, for instance, the CEO of MasterCard, Bob Selander, recognized that a range of disruptive forces could change the game for a company that had held its initial public offering of stock just the year before, and had flourished since then. These potential disruptions included the replacement of credit and debit cards by mobile phones and other electronic devices; possible major changes in regulation; and consolidation in the financial sector. Selander and his team developed a discipline of "dynamic strategy" that continuously engaged the whole organization in scanning the landscape, updating its views of market scenarios and their likelihood, and evaluating whether the time was ripe yet to consider developing a new way to play.

The defense industry in the United States provides another example of how external changes can prompt changes in your way to play while opening up the market to non-traditional competitors. Before 1990, most defense companies were essentially a combination of solution providers and regulation navigators. They were oriented around the Department of Defense's demand for enormously expensive and capable weapons systems targeted at major threats such as the Soviet Union. Then the Berlin Wall fell. Defense acquisitions budgets were cut 50 percent in search of a "peace dividend," and exotic weapons, such as stealth-bomber aircraft and nuclear submarines, were requested in much smaller numbers than had been originally planned. This shift was reinforced by the Al-Qaeda attack on September 11, 2001; massive weapons were of little use against terrorists and insurgencies hiding in caves and deploying improvised explosive devices.

The legacy defense industry had difficulty at first adjusting to the new realities, and non-traditional suppliers filled the gap. For example, U.S. defense-related agencies broadened their procurement strategies to include some overseas producers who already had the right to win for this new market. For example, just about every helicopter purchased since 9/11 by the U.S. Department of Homeland Security (including the U.S. Coast Guard) was built outside the United States, and the U.S. Navy's Littoral surface combat ships were produced in shipyards owned by non-U.S. companies.

At the same time, disruptive weapons technologies began to appear: robots, autonomous systems like the Predator and Global Hawk drones, and the global information grid, which transferred computer intelligence from individual ships, planes, and tanks to the network. All of this value shifted from producers of traditional military hardware to newly arisen network integrators. For example, the Predator drones that hunt insurgents in Afghanistan are guided remotely by pilots sitting in Nevada, and the real-time data these drones collect are analyzed simultaneously in multiple locations in the United States and elsewhere around the world. A new group of defense companies—some with roots in Silicon Valley or the computer industry, and some from outside the United States—sprang up to create and design these technologies. These companies had faster business cycles, new types of product-development strategies for this industry, and a greater willingness to experiment with untested concepts.

With their legacy business facing flat or declining revenues, the established defense companies thus face a challenge. They have to find a way to play that allows them to cut costs on existing projects—with more off-the-shelf commercial components, simpler designs, and more emphasis on everyday use. For example, the Electric Boat Corporation, which is part of General Dynamics, reduced the cost of building a Virginia-class nuclear submarine by half a billion dollars by ripping out unneeded complexity in the design and production.

The non-traditional suppliers also face challenging limits as the Department of Defense continues to refine its priorities. For example, the disruptive suppliers of robots and networking equipment have enjoyed a defense boom, but none of them have yet risen above $1 billion in sales, far below the $20 billion-plus volume of the legacy players.

All of the competitors are looking for ways to embrace the new technologies and business realities—without falling prey to the incoherence that would come from managing two ways to play, the old and the new, at once. Some are meeting this challenge through a concept called *tailored business streams*, in which they act as a systems integrator: pulling together outside technologies and proprietary in-house expertise in real time, to customize weapons systems for a variety of government clients.

Companies leading the way include Oshkosh Truck (a military vehicle manufacturer), Eurocopter (a French/German helicopter producer), and Cisco Systems (in its network equipment business). Some legacy producers are also entering this space through acquisition: for example, Northrop Grumman purchased Teledyne Ryan, the builder of Global Hawk drones. The most astute large incumbents have been careful to not overwhelm their new subsidiaries with incoherent legacy business models. The subsidiaries exist in the short term as discrete businesses, each with a separate way to play and capabilities system, until they can be integrated into the larger company. The companies that are first to master this approach, consolidating their capabilities into a single way to play, will shape the direction of the defense business for years to come.

Your way to play is supported by your capabilities system—and is therefore feasible

The most important criterion for a way to play has to do with your ability to deliver. How well does your capabilities system support this way to play? Rather than picking a market because it is attractive and developing the capabilities to match, pick the market where your capabilities will work. As with Walmart, Target, Apple, and the leading defense companies mentioned in this chapter, it won't be enough to merely have relevant capabilities. They will have to be distinctive, well realized, sophisticated, and backed up by a deep organizational commitment, if your way to play is to be feasible in the real world. We will discuss this important topic of successful capabilities systems in the next chapter.

CHAPTER FIVE

THE CAPABILITIES SYSTEM

When Jeff Bezos launched Amazon.com as "the world's biggest bookstore" in 1995, people took that slogan at face value. Here was a great new way to buy printed reading material. But Bezos knew that books were just an initial proof-point. Music CDs came next, and then Amazon suddenly became a clothing store, a pharmacy, a bicycle shop, an electronics outlet, and a gourmet food emporium—all rolled into one and reachable through your computer. Not everything worked; Amazon's foray into online auctions faltered. But with a culture that tolerated failure as long as it came with learning, Amazon has kept on trying and has succeeded far more often than it has failed. It is an excellent example of a world-class capabilities system as the engine of success.

Amazon's way to play revolves around its role as an experience provider and a superaggregator of vendors and customers, giving people a compelling, one-stop online shopping experience with easy access to products from around the world, information about those products supplied by millions of other customers, and friction-free product delivery. To make this work, Amazon must be perceived as the most trusted location on the Internet and the most central hub for electronic commerce—the hub that everyone thinks of first. In short, Bezos and the Amazon leadership team have updated the mission of the original nineteenth-century department store: vast comparability of items in a wide variety of shopping categories.

Amazon's way to play thus represents an ingenious application of the economic concept of *increasing returns*, also known as the network effect.[1] The greater the number of suppliers and customers that use Amazon as their marketplace of choice, and the more they participate by rating and commenting on each other's wares, the greater the number of new people who are drawn in, thereby making the marketplace even more valuable.

Finally, the way to play also takes account of the reasons people shop in the first place. As Bezos put it, Amazon's customers want "selection, low prices, and fast delivery . . . I can't imagine that ten years from now they are going to say, 'I love Amazon, but if only they could deliver my products a little more slowly' . . . 'Or I wish their prices were a little higher.'"[2] Put together, these features more than compensate for the most challenging aspect of electronic retailing: that consumers can't physically touch merchandise and walk away with it immediately.

A system of five key integrated capabilities supports this complex and highly effective way to play:

Retail interface design: From its earliest days, when it pioneered the inclusion of customer recommendations and in-depth product information on its Web site, Amazon has excelled at retail interface design. The elegant, seamless qualities of the Amazon site—full of detail, but not cluttered, and with highly sophisticated search, comment, linking, and online payment features—have turned the site into an international information utility. It is the free, de facto repository of record for data on the books, media items, and other products that it carries and (increasingly) on the people who create and purchase them. This interface design capability was also tapped for Amazon's Kindle electronic reading device, the first such device to be successful.

Back-end supply chain: This online retailer has also painstakingly developed a back-end supply chain capability that even the operations department at Walmart might envy. It handles massive numbers of products through networks of specialized warehouses and the supply chains of many of its partners. This means that as part of its supply-chain management, Amazon must be able to manage its vendors, to keep customers from being disappointed if the suppliers don't deliver with the same accuracy and speed. That is one reason Amazon also makes its in-house logistics available to its independent suppliers, who get, on average, a 70 percent lift in sales and a 30 percent reduction in returns by switching to the "Fulfilled by Amazon" program. The supply chain is linked closely to the Web site, so that customers can reroute orders on the fly or cancel them until the last moment, with no questions asked.

Merchandising: This capability is Amazon's hidden source of value. Like Target, another consummate merchandiser, Amazon doesn't always have the absolutely best price, but it maintains trust by keeping its average prices lower than those of most other vendors, while managing their assortment of featured items aggressively. Amazon purchasing agents identify attractive products rapidly and work closely with producers to display them in exclusive ways. The Flip Ultra video camera, for example, appeared prominently and profitably on Amazon.com in time for the 2007 Christmas season, because of the online store's proficiency. After a meeting at Amazon's Seattle headquarters, the marketers flew home; when they arrived a few hours later, Amazon already had a live prototype of the Web pages ready, showing images of wedding and baby videos.

Customer-relationship management: Amazon's customer-relationship management capability and the robust analytics underlying it are well known. Visitors rapidly learn about affinities—to others who liked the same product or to other products that they might like themselves—without feeling that their privacy has been broached. This capability also allows Amazon to understand its customers superlatively, for example, to solve customer dissatisfaction issues before they occur, because of its knowledge of what customers have needed in the past. Thus, this capability helps Amazon avoid a reliance on reactive and expensive customer service. Amazon's premium service, called Amazon Prime, gives frequent users steep discounts on fast shipping in exchange for an annual fee and even more intensive analytics and relationship-building.

Technological innovation: A final capability is rapid, experimental, and pragmatic technological innovation, often operating behind the scenes. This capability enabled many of Amazon's leading-edge features and offerings, including the Kindle, the "one-click" instant-ordering system, and its cloud computer services, which were originally designed for Amazon's internal use but have since been extended to customers. Because these computer services can be listed in Amazon's online structure, delivered with little extra expense, and managed with little service or support, Amazon can offer them online to customers in ways that build on and expand its way to play. For example, Amazon's Mechanical Turk brokerage service allows people to post help-wanted notices for very small tasks—such as programming, editing, sorting, or entering comments in social media sites—that others can execute from their computers and get paid for through Amazon. By the time you read this paragraph, the details here may be obsolete, because Amazon will have introduced newly innovated services and features by then.

The strength of these capabilities, as always, is most powerful in the way they come together as a system. Amazon is known for its proficiency at *upselling*—drawing customers to purchase more products per transaction (or online basket) than just about any other company. That's because each transaction combines analytics (identifying the right products of interest for a given consumer) with superior merchandising (delivering those right items at the right prices), with customer management and interface design (coalescing that massive complexity into a simple point-of-purchase opportunity) and supply-chain excellence (delivering on its promise for speed and reliability) to reinforce the moment of truth, when a consumer adds to a purchase. Without any one of those capabilities at world-class levels, Amazon could not have posted its consistent growth rates; even during the 2008–2009 recession, the retailer grew more than 20 percent each quarter. It did this while maintaining gross margins of 18 to 20 percent and offering extremely low prices on many items.

Note that Amazon.com has never built or bought its own brick-and-mortar stores, not even experimentally. Most other companies would have been tempted, but Bezos and his executive team are apparently aware that this would require coming up to speed with a whole new incompatible system of complex capabilities, against a host of more experienced and capable competitors. This way, when brick-and-mortar retail chains build their Web sites, they enter Amazon's turf, where it is already the most coherent, capable player by far.

Amazon's capabilities system has been under development steadily since the mid-1990s. Back in 1999, at the height of the dot-com boom, we recall seeing a television segment about Amazon. The Christmas selling season had begun, and there was Jeff Bezos, standing in a distribution center, wearing a hard hat and discussing the automatic sort, pick, and pack machines that his company had started using. At a time when other dot-com executives were talking about "eyeballs" and "frictionless commerce," Bezos's priorities seemed startlingly un-"e"-like. But in the years since, as our Amazon orders have arrived when we expected, with never a mistake, and as Amazon's revenue has grown by a factor of ten, we've often been reminded of the clarity of his thinking.

Amazon continues to develop all its capabilities—both organically and through acquisitions. (In chapter 8, we'll look more closely at Amazon's capabilities-driven acquisition of Zappos, the online apparel store.) One of the most telling examples is Amazon's launch of same-day delivery in ten major U.S. cities during the summer of 2010. Having made some online supermarket acquisitions, the retailer discovered the value of local delivery fleets and rapidly integrated those with the rest of its logistics. This also enables extra features, such as Saturday delivery, that can attract new Amazon Prime members. The company is now using its well-honed analytics to decide where to offer what types of same-day delivery, and to whom. Other companies, like Webvan (which Amazon purchased after its 2001 bankruptcy), have failed spectacularly in this field, but Amazon may well succeed.

The Distinctive Capability

As we explained earlier, a capability is not simply a function or practice. It is the ability to reliably and consistently deliver a specified outcome, in support of your way to play. This capability is ensured through the right combination of processes, tools, knowledge, skills, and organization, all focused on meeting the desired result. The most important capabilities are distinctive: each of them represents an extraordinary competence that few others can master.

When they hear the word *capabilities*, many businesspeople think of intangible assets: employees' skill sets or the quality of work done by a corporate function such as R&D or supply chain. Others associate it with the competency models administered by human resources departments or with learning and development efforts. But we use the term in a more specific and strategy-related way: capabilities are the defining strengths that your company must have to help it compete.

Gary Hamel and C. K. Prahalad amplify that definition usefully in their book *Competing for the Future*. Using the term *core competence*, they define a capability as a "bundle of skills and technologies that enables a company to provide a particular benefit to customers."[3] To Hamel and Prahalad, a core competence has a clear, customer-perceived benefit and a competitive advantage, and it can be extended to other products and markets. They argue—correctly, in our view—that it falls to senior management to identify the core competencies of a company, to continue to strengthen those competencies, and to invest in new ones. Senior management must also make sure that core competencies don't get trapped in the silos of business units.

As the experience of companies like Amazon suggests, a single capability can take years to develop, drawing upon a range of people (and their skills and knowledge), as well as embodying processes, technologies, and practices. The more distinctive that capability and the more related to your way to play, the more valuable it is.

Capabilities can include anything a company does with distinction to realize its way to play. They need not be directly visible to outsiders: Amazon's behind-the-scenes merchandising capability, which is critical to its success, is hardly noted by most observers. Capabilities don't have to be private-sector-specific. For an employment agency with public-sector clients, recruiting and developing people for government work may be a critical capability. For a protected utility, a state-owned enterprise, or an organization competing in some developing economies, managing government relationships could matter more than any kind of specific marketing acumen.

The way you think about capabilities is important because it can shape the way you conceive of and build them. For example, some executives look at capabilities so vaguely (e.g., thinking of quality, innovation, consumer insight, or supply-chain management as capabilities) that investments in these capabilities can mean almost anything. These are generally important functions; every large company invests in them. But there are dozens of ways to excel at innovation, and many of them are specific to particular product categories, industries, and even regions. A new motor-vehicle launch program would require very different skills and supply-chain methods depending on whether it's a truck or a microcar; a gasoline- or electric-powered vehicle; or a launch in India, China, Europe, or the United States. If you don't have a clear sense of what types of innovation are included in your capability and what types are not, then you haven't defined it rigorously enough.

Capabilities Versus Assets

Many corporate leaders assign insufficient weight to their differentiating capabilities in developing strategy. Instead, they base their strategy on an assessment of their assets—their patents, brands, land, facilities, machinery, supplier and customer connections, and cash. Guided in part by this "asset-forward" view of the world, they tend to compete most heavily wherever they have assets at sufficient scale.

That's shortsighted. If assets were the primary factor underlying success, then any company in an industry could win by adopting the same strategy, as long as it had enough capital to buy the assets it needed. Moreover, assets tend to depreciate in value and can diminish unexpectedly. For example, the value of patents expires, and in many sectors, it has become easier to manage around them.

A capability, by contrast, is yours. It can't be stolen or easily bought by competitors; by the time they copy what you know how to do, you will already have evolved the capability further. Even if they duplicate some of your methods, they will not be able to make use of them as you do.

Honeywell realized this in its operations in China several years ago, when it successfully introduced a new line of thermostats and control devices for Chinese buildings and industries. Other technology manufacturers, entering China with the assets of their technologies (and, in some cases, their patents), had been confronted by Chinese knockoff producers, which essentially counterfeited their devices and sold them at lower cost. Instead, Honeywell opened a new R&D center in Shanghai, employing two thousand, to develop its subsequent products for the Chinese market—and to back up those products with support and services that no knockoff producer could easily duplicate. Within three years, the company tripled its revenues in China.[4]

Fixed assets are more difficult to apply across many products, services, and businesses than are capabilities, which further limits fixed assets' value. Moreover, even the most valuable and long-lived assets are, increasingly, table stakes in most competitive industries. Everyone in the game has to have them, but they are rarely the basis of sustainable differentiation, because anyone with capital can acquire them.

Time favors the capabilities-driven strategy over the asset-driven strategy. While assets depreciate, the value of a capability tends to grow as it is used and improved. Consider the difference between an oil company strategy based on exploiting the oil fields it already owns (its assets), versus a strategy aimed at expanding the ability to safely discover and develop new fields (a capability that generates new assets). Many types of capabilities can also be used to develop new assets. An improved innovation capability will lead a company to hold more patents (and more profitable patents). A strong marketing capability sustains the viability of a brand.

We do not suggest that you ignore assets; they play a major role in how you go to market. But the power of an effective capability can surprise you. We recall a conversation with leaders of a large European food company, in which they talked about the distribution network that they used to deliver prepared meats. Suddenly, one of the top executives looked up and said, "I didn't realize this before. But nobody else understands how to transport a sausage to the shelf this way." Sausage distribution, hardly the company's main business, had always seemed trivial, but suddenly the executives realized that this specific distribution capability could be applied to a wide range of other food products, where local tastes and freshness were important customer requirements. If they invested in it properly and applied it more broadly, it could lead to some entirely new growth opportunities.

The Capabilities System

A capabilities system consists of the three to six capabilities that distinguish a company and that the company invests in; these capabilities reinforce one another in the service of the company's way to play. To put it more broadly, the capabilities system is the integrated group of activities that enables a company to create value in the path it has chosen. Every great company, we believe, is supported by a well-established, well-supported, and focused system of capabilities.

The value of a capabilities system has not always been recognized by business thinkers as it should be. One who did recognize it was the eminent strategy writer and business historian Alfred D. Chandler, Jr. "The competitive strengths of industrial firms rest on learned organizational capabilities . . .," he wrote. "Once a new enterprise's competitive power has been tested, its set of integrated organizational capabilities becomes a learning base for improving existing products and processes and for developing new ones."[5] The most successful companies, he added, were those that continued to reinvest their earnings in improving their capabilities, bringing them together, and deploying them against competitors.[6]

As Chandler acknowledged in an interview in 2001, this concept summed up his lifelong effort to understand why some enterprises were influential in shaping their industry, while others withered. Born in 1918 into the du Pont and Poor (of Standard & Poor's) families, he had grown up in the heart of emergent business culture, and he had begun his quest as a teenager, poring over old railroad expense records that he had found in his great-aunt's attic. Along the way he wrote a series of seminal books, including *Strategy and Structure: Chapters in the History of the American Industrial Enterprise* (1962), the first to lay out a concept of business strategy as a long-term group of goals and objectives, and *The Visible Hand: The Managerial Revolution in American Business* (1977), which was the first business book to win the Pulitzer Prize.[7] He also founded the academic field of business history, as a professor at Harvard University.

But it wasn't until his last two books—*Inventing the Electronic Century* (2001), on consumer and computer electronics, and *Shaping the Industrial Century* (2005), on chemicals and pharmaceuticals—that Chandler came to feel that he had cracked the code of business success, and the evolution of industries as well. In these books, both published shortly before he died in 2007, he followed story after story of business competition. The company that reinvested in its own capabilities invariably won the market. One of many examples was IBM versus Sperry Rand in 1953, both making the transition from tabulating machines to computers. Sperry Rand had a three-year head start, but according to Chandler, its teams squabbled, its sales force had little interest in the new products from R&D, and its leadership was reluctant to invest in either technology or human skills. IBM, led by Thomas Watson, Sr., focused intently on building and applying its capabilities in hardware and software. It applied its experience with punch card tabulators, for example, to design peripherals for its new computers. The 650 mainframe, launched in 1954 and later dubbed "computing's Model T" by Watson himself, was the source of immense revenue, which the company plowed back into furthering both its technical and its sales capabilities.[8] Chandler argued that the "integrated learning base" (his phrase for a capabilities system) created enough of an advantage to enable companies to outperform competitors for decades—or until they stopped reinvesting in it.

In a coherent company, a capabilities system is the chosen vehicle for channeling investment. It establishes a new form of scale by deploying capabilities more broadly. As we've seen with Pfizer Consumer Healthcare, JCI, and the food company described in chapter 4, designing a capabilities system also serves as a natural way to align people's thinking. It was not just the capabilities individually that were essential, but how they operated in a system. Each capabilities system, in fact, requires capabilities that are well matched—just as a high-performance sports car requires a high-performance engine, transmission, and tires that are very different from those you would install on a pickup truck. A capabilities system must also be well matched to your way to play; it provides a powerful basis for choosing a successful way to play for your company.

Companies that combine capabilities into a system gain tremendous advantage over their competitors. Another good example is Inditex, the Spanish fashion manufacturer and retailer, better known by its main brand name, Zara. Zara's remarkable success depends on combining seemingly unrelated capabilities in customer insight, rapid-response manufacturing innovation, logistics, and nimble fashion design. These all come together in a very specific way.

If you walk into a Zara retail store, you'll find some "classic" garments, which change infrequently; these are outsourced to manufacturers from low-wage countries like Sri Lanka and Malaysia. Seasonal and fashion-forward clothes are produced at Zara's own factories and suppliers in Europe, where the company has built the remarkable capability of redesigning clothes quickly in response to analysis and insight. Kaj Grichnik and Conrad Winkler describe this rapid process in their book *Make or Break*:

> The production cycle is kept short and intensely responsive to information gathered from retail stores—about which products shoppers buy, what they try on, whether they have problems with zippers or fit, and what they request . . . Zara's rapid-fire designers can produce a new garment in response to consumer demand within a few weeks, put it out in the trend line, and then—if consumer interest so dictates—move it to one of the other, slower-moving product lines. The interchange among data from the store, decisions made by the designers, fabrication, and distribution is nearly seamless—and is improving all the time.[9]

Zara's full price is often 15 percent below the full prices of specialty competitors, and its assortment is well-managed. Because its purposefully changing inventory and everyday lower prices attract customers, it does not need to discount as heavily as other retailers do. Day by day, it sells a higher proportion of its clothing than do competitors at regular prices—and about 20 percent more units per square foot of retail space. This provides more value to the consumer than the traditional method of marking down items for discounts when they are no longer new, with a much more profitable cost structure for the company. In fact, it's a mutually reinforcing benefit. The more the capabilities system provides the right assortment in the right quantities, the more Zara can pass that value (in lower working capital, fewer markdowns, and less written-off inventory) to customers. This in turn provides more scale for the capabilities system, as consumers come back more often, looking for the next iteration of style. Even when other clothing manufacturers and retailers have struggled with shrinking profit margins, Zara reports consistent growth in earnings. Moreover, because of the close alignment among its capabilities, the system is almost impossible to copy.

Another example is Frito-Lay, the snack division of PepsiCo. Three basic integrated capabilities, involving human and physical capital, fit within its system. The first is direct store delivery (DSD). On several continents, Frito-Lay, rather than relying on a third-party distributor, has its own fleets of trucks with skilled and motivated drivers who are known for their ability to build relations with store owners, commandeer shelf space, and even offer stores credit. (The DSD network provides limited banking services in some markets.) Frito-Lay actually invented the handheld computer to enable its DSD capability.

To be sure, DSD is not considered a highly differentiated capability today. Many consumer packaged-goods companies distribute merchandise this way. But in its use of information technology, training, and skilled global management, Frito-Lay still maintains a clear, distinct advantage in getting the right product to the right place at the right time. More importantly, Frito-Lay parlays it in combination with two other distinctive capabilities: the continuous innovation of new products (particularly new flavors), and a proficiency with local consumer marketing programs that reinforce demand.

Like Zara, Frito-Lay has built a value chain that would be very difficult for another company to replicate, because these three capabilities work so well together. For example, it deploys them to rapidly and broadly test new products in the market. Most consumer packaged-goods companies struggle with market tests of new products, because they rely on retailers to stock the shelves; the associated slotting fees can add up to $1 to $2 million for a new product in the United States.

But Frito-Lay stocks its own products. This gives it tremendous cost savings and the flexibility to launch and test new products. If the products don't attract customers, Frito-Lay can withdraw them quickly. If the products are hits, that's even better; because it "owns the shelf," there's a direct link back to innovation and marketing. It can rapidly build demand, which reinforces the relationship with retail grocers.

Closing the Capabilities Gap

In chapter 10, we'll discuss the design of a capabilities system and its continual refinement over time. But even at the very first stages, one question should be at the heart of your thinking: what is the gap between the capabilities you will need and the capabilities you already have?

Your way to play should largely be developed in light of the capabilities you already have. It should take into account everything you're great at. But inevitably, given the incoherence of the past and the ambitions of the present, there will be gaps you'll have to fill. Indeed, the gaps may sometimes be so great that you will find it challenging to earn a right to win. You may even need to reconsider your chosen way to play. (In chapter 10, we'll discuss how to evaluate these gaps in light of your competitors.)

Several snack companies are now facing this type of dilemma. Health and wellness are widespread trends, and many food manufacturers are investing heavily in innovative, health-based new products. But within these companies, there's a backlash of people who are quite reasonably asking if the companies can fulfill their promises. These companies have well-honed capabilities bringing to market the salty, sugary snacks that trigger emotional connections with people. As the companies add healthier food products to the mix, they are having difficulty creating value. They are trying to support two ways to play at one time, each way requiring a very different type of R&D and marketing, and their capabilities systems may not be up to the challenge.

In similar circumstances, you don't necessarily have to settle for incoherence. You do need to be more explicit about the stretch required to accomplish your new way to play. Look closely at the companies that have the greatest right to win in that new business. What capabilities are they bringing to bear?

Then assess your own capabilities in the light of your distinction. What could you do better than anyone else in this arena? Conversely, what would it take to develop or acquire the capabilities you need to win in this new way to play? Would you need to acquire technology? Train and develop people in new ways? Invest in R&D differently? Build new types of practices and create new policies? Where does the expertise related to these capabilities exist—inside your firm or outside, or both?

In assessing your capabilities gap, look at the capabilities that you aren't using fully. For example, you may have invested heavily in a supply chain or legal capability that has only paid off in one or two product lines. These should either be extended to your full company (if they prove valuable there), or the investment should be reconsidered.

Also consider the measures required to deploy the same capabilities against many parts of your business. Will the staff and processes involved be the same? If not, how do they interact? Will the handoff from one capability to the next be designed by a single team? Or do you want people within the relevant functions and business practices to conceive and develop their parts of it cross-functionally?

The relevance of your capabilities to your business, of course, is not just an operational issue. The next chapter focuses on this third strategic element: the lineup of products and services in your company, and the degree to which they fit with both your capabilities system and your way to play.

CHAPTER SIX

PRODUCT AND SERVICE FIT

At any level—from regional office to division to enterprise—a company's most visible aspects to its customers and the rest of the outside world are its products and services. It's not surprising that most companies define themselves this way: "We are a car company," managers say, introducing their firms. "We are a phone company." "We sell accounting services." Even companies that migrate to other businesses in a coherent manner still retain their original identity: IBM and Apple are still referred to as "computer makers," and Disney as a "cartoon company," even though all three companies do so much more with the same capabilities system.

Internally, product and service categories are even more closely tied to a company's identity. Companies count their revenues and costs accordingly, thereby reinforcing the roster of products and services as the company's organizational spine. This is a natural thing to do, but it has unfortunate side effects. Instead of differentiating you, it sets you up with the same structure as just about every other company in your industry. It amplifies the incoherence penalty, with its costs and inefficiencies. It makes it more difficult to align your products and services with your capabilities system, and it adds pervasive pressure to design your strategy to fit your existing portfolio. Finally, it makes your business more risky—if the market changes for your flagship products, where do you go?

If instead you define your company by its way to play and capabilities system, it will be much easier to differentiate yourself, gain the coherence premium, and adapt to market changes without a blow to your identity. Doing this, however, means a shift in perspective about your products and services. Now, their value potential depends primarily on their relevance to your strategy instead of the other way around. You judge your lineup of products and services based not so much on their individual potential, but on coherence: on their strategic fit with your capabilities system and way to play.

Unfortunately, many companies don't pay much attention to the coherence of the business—or the impact that their lineup of products and services can have on it. In many companies, the idea of fit is associated with being in the same sector. Two automobiles, or two food products, are automatically assumed to fit together naturally, whether or not they depend on similar capabilities systems. This view leads many companies to expand to adjacencies: products and services that seem related, but that may require very different capabilities to win. (In chapter 7, we'll go into more detail on the adjacency trap.) That's why we typically advise executives to form a very clear idea of their way to play and capabilities system before making decisions about products and services—and to line up products and services, not with one another, but with the firm's overall strategy.

When products and services do not fit into your way to play or capabilities system, you can end up with immense costs and inefficiencies. These often arise when you try to make the most of a constrained investment pool, spreading it around on too many offerings. Somewhere out there, you may have a competitor that is more coherent than you, investing in fewer capabilities to support a better-fitting lineup of products and services—and therefore beating you in the market, time and time again. You have probably seen this happen already in some parts of your business. And while these businesses pay the cost of failure, the largest price of this incoherence is paid by the parts of the businesses that do fit, but that do not get the investment and attention they require.

Frankly, if you can't find a way to align some of your products and services with your capabilities system and way to play, then maybe you shouldn't be in those businesses. Maybe you should divest them, and in the process release short-term capital to reinvest in the more coherent parts of your company.

In this chapter, we present the practice of portfolio analysis from a coherence perspective. At the enterprise level, the word "portfolio" typically means the lineup of businesses and business units, but within individual businesses, we also mean your specific lineup of products and services. It can also mean the portfolio of R&D projects or line extensions that you are considering. All of these have the potential to increase either coherence or incoherence, depending on the choices you make.

Listerine PocketPaks: When Terrific Products Don't Fit

The story of the rise and fall of Listerine PocketPaks shows how a breakthrough product or service can fail if the right way to play and capabilities system aren't there to support it. As we saw in chapter 1, the leaders of Pfizer Consumer Healthcare (PCH), which owned Listerine, navigated nearly every product and service decision they made in favor of coherence. They primarily favored products that fit their capabilities system and could deliver on health-related claims. One of their few missteps was the Listerine PocketPak, rolled out in the early 2000s.

PocketPaks were the first breath-freshening dissolvable film strips produced in the United States. Adapted from a Japanese product, they are edible, paper-thin strips that melt on the tongue and deliver a dose of flavor. Listerine's mouthwash-releasing "breath strips," as they were called, were a runaway hit with a blockbuster brand, genuine appeal, and an immediate business success story. As the first to market, Pfizer enjoyed a first-mover bonanza, with $160 million in sales in the product's first full year.[1] *Time* magazine hailed PocketPaks as one of the breakthrough inventions of 2002.[2]

The PCH managers saw the product as a natural fit: an extension of their Listerine mouthwash brand. They tried to apply their company's differentiating capabilities, such as claims-based marketing. But a health-benefits-based marketing approach conferred no major advantage to a product that was, in the end, a confection. It needed to be sold in the racks near the cashier, alongside gums and candies, and it relied on constant flavor innovation to maintain its popularity.

Thus, Pfizer's commanding market position proved brief. By 2004, competitors had introduced more than a dozen new breath-strip brands. The most prominent rival was Eclipse Flash Strips, produced by the Wrigley gum company. This was the first nongum product in Wrigley's 113-year history; the company was attracted to this business in part because breath-strip popularity was cutting into sugar-free gum sales. Its Eclipse brand put out four flavors—cinnamon, peppermint, wintergreen, and spearmint—before Listerine could get its second flavor to the shelf. Eclipse rapidly overtook Listerine to become the number one breath strip on the market.[3]

As a chewing gum company, Wrigley had a confectionary-oriented capabilities system that Pfizer lacked; this system included expertise in capturing space on the candy racks and rapid-cycle flavor innovation. That was enough to prevail, despite the first mover's early and overwhelming lead, and despite the enormous asset of the Listerine brand.

Ironically, dissolvable strips may ultimately prove to fit better with a claims-oriented capabilities system like Listerine's, after all—but for a different group of products. The strips are resurfacing today as vehicles for delivering medicine, especially for animals and children who find it hard to swallow pills.[4]

You may have your own similar products or services—offerings too innovative or cherished to give up, but not at all aligned to your capabilities system. You may not be able to make them belong. What do you do? Work your way methodically through each of your products and services. Test them to see if you are equipped to take them to the customer in a way that gives you a meaningful and sustainable right to win. And decide their fate accordingly.

The Capabilities-Driven Portfolio

For the company seeking coherence, conventional portfolio decision tools can be misleading. The growth-share portfolio management matrix, developed by the Boston Consulting Group in the 1960s, made it easy for corporate strategists to categorize each business, product, or service according to its market share (indicating position relative to the competition) and market growth (indicating changes in the number of customers for the overall category). The most attractive quadrant, labeled "stars," has the highest growth and highest share. These are the primary candidates for investment. Other businesses with high market share, the "cows," are kept and milked, while the slow-growth, low-share "dogs" are relegated to be sold or abandoned. This was extremely valuable when market growth and market share were distinctive attributes and predictive in themselves of success. Since then, many other portfolio frameworks have been developed, mostly focusing on financial metrics—which is understandable, given the continuous need for short-term performance results.[5]

But today, it can be dangerous to base portfolio decisions primarily on growth, market share, or other short-term financial metrics, especially if you don't take coherence and capabilities into account. Invest in that "star" product line that has been growing for two years at 19 percent per annum? You may be better off passing on it in favor of a "dog" that's growing at 3 percent a year, if the slower-growing business is coherent with your way to play and your capabilities system.[6] The problem is the metrics, which often provide misleading valuations. They don't take into account, for example, what the "star" might be worth to your company if you sold it to another company with a better-matched capabilities system, or the hidden costs of continued investment in an incoherent product or service line.

Nor do the metrics show what value could be created if the "dogs" received the support they need, and could make use of your differentiating capabilities. This in fact has been an ongoing, much-noted problem with most forms of the growth-share matrix. Critics of those matrices, writes strategy historian Walter Kiechel, have "especially delighted in examples of low-share, low-growth businesses that, when taken under new management, ended up being gratifyingly profitable."[7] This hidden potential value is generally not manifest in market share, which is a lagging indicator, at best, of coherence.

Even more advanced forms of financial valuation don't include the value of future coherence. They implicitly assume that a company's coherence will stay the same, reflecting whatever way to play and capabilities are in place currently, no matter what plans for change exist. These forms of valuation don't challenge the current business model or show how a business might perform with greater coherence. They also reveal very little about the potential incoherence penalty of the enterprise: the costs and distractions that stem from not focusing on a single way to play with one capabilities system. Moreover, they do not consider alternatives; they do not drive managers to ask how much a business or product line would be worth if it were sold to another company that could apply a more coherent model to it.

Many companies have begun to recognize this and now include a "fitness" metric now in their portfolio analysis. This is a good first step, but the prevailing definitions of "fit" still tend to be misleading. Most of them have to do with adjacency: whether the products or services reside within the same sector. In other words, businesses are judged according to whether they fit the definition of "what we sell," rather than "what sets us apart." Moreover, the question of strategic fit is typically raised at the end of a strategic planning process, when the team has already come to its conclusions about performance and is beginning to act on them. At such times, the temptation to force-fit the answer that people want to hear is hard to resist.

It's better to analyze your product and service fit earlier in any planning process. We recommend the portfolio analysis shown in figure 6-1. Use it to judge your potential market value more effectively, to proactively create portfolio value instead of merely balancing the components you have, and to bring your enterprise into greater alignment. It can also be used to evaluate acquisition opportunities (see chapter 8).

In this figure, y-axis (value) represents a forward-looking assessment of a product, service, or business unit. You can use enterprise value or equity value (subtracting net debt from enterprise value) for this purpose, deriving them from estimated future profits (net of capital costs) or future cash flow. (All of these metrics assume no change in the underlying coherence of the business.)

To assess coherence on the x-axis, quantify the extent to which your capabilities system is used as a differentiator for each of the businesses, as we did in chapter 2. Or you may bring a group of senior leaders together and consider each of the businesses in turn.

FIGURE 6-1

A portfolio matrix for gaining coherence

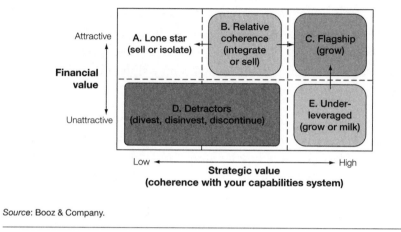

Source: Booz & Company.

Your businesses will fall into five groups:

A. These "lone stars," with low coherence but high financial value, are clearly worth a great deal—but may be worth more to another company than to you. There's an incoherence penalty for keeping them, because they require investment unrelated to the rest of your portfolio. Look for opportunities to monetize them. Build them up to sell them at the appropriate time (as Pfizer did with PCH), rethink your way to play so that you can include them, or treat them as a stand-alone small business (as Procter & Gamble does with Pringles potato chips). By moving early, you can sell at a propitious time, when there are more alternatives and when you have a prospect generally recognized as valuable, rather than after the business has begun to lose value when a stronger, disruptive competitor has emerged.

B. These businesses have relative coherence: they outperform the competition, but they are only partly aligned to your way to play and capabilities system. Hang on to these businesses and invest in them, if all three of the following conditions are true: (1) you expect them to keep outperforming competitors, because the capabilities system they deploy will continue to be relevant to customers; (2) the capabilities system that supports them overlaps with the differentiated capabilities—not the table stakes—of your primary business; and (3) when you look into monetizing them, the potential sale price is unattractive. Otherwise, divest. If you keep these businesses, you'll have to watch them carefully; the world may shift and their relative advantage may rapidly disappear.

C. This group contains your most promising endeavors—the "flagship" businesses with high coherence and high financial value. They are already your stars—or should be. As we'll see in chapter 7, you may create ways to accentuate their growth and flagship business status.

D. The detractors are businesses with low financial value and low coherence that drag your company down and constitute a major source of the incoherence penalty. Your first concern is to stop them from hemorrhaging cash. Next, figure out why they are doing so poorly. You may end up selling them at a reasonable price, isolating them from the rest of your enterprise while optimizing their performance for cash, or discontinuing them if necessary. Like the businesses in group A, they may be worth more to others; look for likely buyers that can create more value than your capabilities system allows.

E. With high coherence but low financial value, these businesses may well be among the "dogs" of a conventional analysis. But they also represent your most underleveraged (and underappreciated) opportunities. Will additional investment in these businesses, or greater linkage to your capabilities system, propel them to earn a right to win? If so, and if you are prepared to invest in them more heavily, move them into the C group. If not, milk them—either for cash or for the support they offer your capabilities system and other businesses—until they are ready to be sold or shut down.

Whether these are business units, products, services, or other parts of your portfolio, the same general principle applies: they are always better served when aligned to your chosen capabilities system. With that principle in mind, you can work your way methodically through the list, deciding how each item fits—and where it is best suited to thrive. (You can also apply similar logic to potential acquisitions, as we'll see in chapter 8.)

Rethinking the Portfolio at Ahlstrom

The Ahlstrom company is a good example of a company that reevaluated its products and services in line with coherence and is reaping the benefits. Founded in 1851, Ahlstrom is a $1.6 billion Finnish manufacturer of fiber-based rolled goods, including composites and specialty papers. Its materials are used around the world to make a wide variety of products: turbine blades, boat hulls, masking tape, filters, baby wipes, medical gowns, teabags, sausage casing, wine labels, milk carton paper, building materials, and disposable hygiene products among them. Like many business-to-business companies, Ahlstrom was deeply affected by the economic downturn of 2008–2009. Even in its earliest stages, the downturn was significant enough that CEO Jan Lång, with the approval of the board, initiated an exercise in 2009 to rethink the company's corporate strategy and portfolio of businesses.

The problem, as Lång saw it, was that Ahlstrom hadn't clearly settled on "the reason for being one company": the logic that held the firm together as one group. It had a large and complex line of businesses, built partly through acquisition and spanning a variety of industries, products, technologies, and organizational structures. It was also a highly innovative company; almost half of its net sales in 2009 were generated by new or improved products. But while some product lines were highly profitable or first in market share in their categories, others were struggling. To avoid ongoing losses, the company needed to focus on the businesses that had the most potential within its portfolio and use that to improve operations, and perhaps add other businesses that would make more strategic sense.

To evaluate dozens of product lines, the Ahlstrom executives first defined twenty product groups that made up distinctive businesses and reflected the way their products were used. They then surveyed several hundred customers in fifty countries about the purchasing criteria that had led each customer to select a particular supplier. The survey responses directly or indirectly indicated the capabilities most relevant to each broad product group. The analysis also confirmed what some members of the management team already suspected: some capabilities, such as basic product quality and delivery competence, were merely table stakes. Every supplier had mastered them. Other factors were more distinctive: innovation, technical support, and price; customers made choices most frequently based on these.

In the conversations that followed, Lång and the executive team concluded that their company naturally divided into two categories of business, each with its own capabilities system and way to play. They went down their list of products and services, dividing them into two groups. The first group—including glass-fiber tissue; vegetable parchment; industrial, medical, and food nonwovens; and more—was called "value-added businesses." These were businesses where the technical-support capability was given a strong focus; Ahlstrom's staff typically learned the ins and outs of the customers' production processes and could thus offer those customers specifically tailored assistance for improving their products. These businesses had often built strong relationships with customers in precisely that way. They were tagged for growth and expansion, including possible small acquisitions.

The second group—which included abrasive and coated papers, air filtration, and pre-impregnated décor papers (for the production of laminates)—had not performed as consistently well, but its businesses shared a viable way to play as value players. Here, technical support was rarely needed or requested; price was the primary consideration for most purchasers. These businesses would henceforth focus on improving operational excellence so they could offer more price-competitive products, and on innovating for cost improvement and simplifying the value chain, while the company would allocate most of its growth-oriented investment to the capabilities system of the value-added group.

This was not just another restructuring exercise. With the full executive team involved, Ahlstrom had in effect simplified its line of products into two groups, roughly equivalent to "flagship" and "relative coherence," according to their respective ways to play. Now, all decisions around investment, capability development, and organizational design could be made more simply, with a clear underlying rationale. Since the new strategy was announced, Ahlstrom has designed a new operating model that supports the roles of the two different business clusters and enables corporate functions, including sales and marketing and product and technology development, to more efficiently serve and strengthen the individual businesses. Moreover, a series of growth initiatives is being launched in the value-added businesses. The company is also reorganizing its supply chain and innovation functions to support this group: specifically, to improve product performance and conversion processes for its customers.

As this story shows, a clear look at your product and service lineup can lead to substantial movement toward coherence. Conversely, sooner or later, any company moving toward coherence will reach a similar point of choice about its lineup. The clearer your way to play and the better developed your capabilities system, the easier your task will be.

The Divested Star

One critical part of your capabilities-driven strategy will be selling or streamlining the businesses that do not fit well with your capabilities system and way to play. Selling has several advantages: it removes a distraction, improves the ability of the remaining enterprise to create value, and puts the divested business into a better environment, where it is more likely to thrive. The more value you create from divestiture, the more effectively you can invest in the capabilities that are important to your strategy.

You may be challenged by the notion of selling profitable businesses. Is it really appropriate to get rid of your lone stars, especially since they are reasonably good performers? Although they are probably better off elsewhere, it is very difficult to act on that awareness. A chemical company we know of, for example, owns one disjointed food business through an acquisition. As a small enterprise with a best-selling condiment, this food maker has just enough capabilities to keep the business on track. Its competition is equally ill equipped to move the category forward, and therefore, this food product is financially successful enough that the company keeps reinvesting in it. But in their thoughtful moments, the business leaders are the first to admit that they don't really know how to grow that business into its full potential. Such businesses may be stars, but they are also often deceptively inefficient; they require hidden resources disproportionate to their size and influence, simply because they don't fit with the capabilities needed for other businesses.

We don't care how big or powerful a company may be; it can't do everything. There will always be choices and trade-offs: every business wants to expand its share, each function seeks to build its own world-class capabilities system, and every product or service may be seen as important. But without enough coherence, the decisions about which offerings to support become random, rather than connected to a common strategy. A true capabilities-driven strategy will help you and others throughout your company make those hard decisions in a much easier way.

III

CREATING VALUE

CHAPTER SEVEN

UNLOCKING GROWTH

Around 2003, Walmart hit a wall. The retail chain found itself in a difficult position, one that any company that has reached a $250 billion sales mark might expect, but the difficulty was new to this enterprise. Walmart was having trouble increasing its revenues.

There were several reasons for this. For one, far fewer of its preferred customers were left for Walmart to reach in North America, especially given some daunting local challenges (including community protests) when it tried to open new stores. Moving to other parts of the world was also challenging; the chain had successfully entered the United Kingdom through acquisition (of the ASDA supermarket chain), but it failed to get a foothold in Germany or Japan, despite heavy investment.[1] Back in the United States, in their efforts to build revenue, Walmart's leaders had fallen into the conventional retail game of promotion-based pricing: special sales of discounted products. This hurt its well-known claim, linked to its way to play, of everyday low prices. And executing this new game involved new endeavors—in supplier relations, coupon-related promotion, and remerchandising the store, for example—which did not fit well with the chain's overall capabilities system. In fact, same-store sales in many categories had actually started shrinking, an important and worrisome indicator of the poor health of the retail chain's base business.

Walmart's leaders apparently considered new retail formats—premium stores or neighborhood convenience shops, like 7-Eleven and Tesco. They actually opened about 150 "neighborhood markets," but these experimental formats didn't share the same capabilities system that worked in the main Walmart stores, and thus, at least in the short term, the attempt couldn't provide the growth that the business demanded.

That left one main option to pursue growth: by boosting sales within existing stores. For example, they could try to get Walmart shoppers to return to the store more often, instead of visiting other stores, like supermarkets. Though this might seem like an obvious and critically important thing to do in retail, it is very challenging, which is why most retailers rely on new store openings as their fuel for growth. Walmart already had hundreds of initiatives in place to boost same-store sales—trying to get more foot traffic into the stores and more consumers to "cross the aisle" (as retailers put it) from the clothing racks to the grocery shelves, or vice versa. Energetic and creative as these marketing initiatives were, they weren't driving a lot of new business. If anything, they were further confusing consumers and distracting Walmart from what it did best.

Thus, to grow further and remain coherent, Walmart had to develop a better understanding of why it had reached a plateau in the first place. Was it simply that it had run out of markets to penetrate? Or was there some aspect of its own approach that the leaders could change?

They started by taking a fresh look at the retailer's capabilities system—at what it already did well. For instance, they refined Walmart's already-sophisticated capability in customer insight, segmenting stores by such criteria as local ethnicity, income, prevailing stage of life, level of urbanization, and competition from other retailers. One Walmart store might be located in a mixed-income rural area; another near a golf course catering to retirees; another within a quarter mile of a rapidly growing elementary school; and a fourth in a working-class suburban town. Now each of those stores was given a different store layout and merchandise mix, and sales increased accordingly.

Another breakthrough came from rethinking some merchandise categories. One key to picking up market share in retail is focusing on "switchers": customers who are not 100 percent loyal and will shift their business to whichever store meets their needs most effectively. Walmart discovered some switching opportunities in consumer electronics. This was already a major draw for customers who appreciated the benefits that Walmart, with its capabilities system, could provide best: price savings and reliable brands, especially in audio, television, cameras, video games, and other consumer-oriented items.

To attract more switchers from other stores, the retailer changed its merchandise mix, applying those same well-refined customer insights. In suburban locations, where there were many competitors selling personal computers, Walmart deemphasized those products and focused on consumer electronics. But it kept the personal computer line strong in rural areas, where customers had access to fewer technology retailers and valued the guidance that Walmart could provide. The chain also changed the makeup of its staff and its mix of brand-name products and went back to basics on pricing: no complicated discounts or private-label house brands. By reapplying its powerful capabilities in a category where they fit so well, Walmart created a distinctive, low-priced electronics department that could compete effectively even against more specialized chains like Circuit City (which tried but failed to match Walmart's value play).

In the rest of the store, there were similar changes. The company simplified the store experience dramatically, cutting out many display racks and making the stores look less like supermarkets. Since display racks connote special sales, this change helped Walmart return to its everyday-low-prices approach. The move also lowered labor costs, as constantly changing those goods required a huge effort. It also showed that Walmart could resist the temptation of conventional practice, since these display racks had one of the highest lift (sales increase) factors in the industry.

In another step, executives reduced the number of growth initiatives to tens from hundreds. They promoted fewer products and did it more assiduously, targeting promotions to the particular needs and interests of people in each store. This simplified approach made it easier for managers to learn what was working and to share it with their peers. They applied their capabilities system to a select few new offerings: not just electronics, but contact lenses, a limited assortment of fresh fruit and vegetables, pharmacies, and mobile phones. These changes allowed Walmart to take market share from competitors and reminded customers of the value of its everyday-low-prices proposition.[2]

Walmart's results since 2008 show the growth value of a differentiated capabilities system and a clear way to play. The company's sales productivity jumped. In early 2009, Walmart reported an unexpectedly large 5.1 percent rise in sales at stores open at least a year. Some of this may have been related to the 2008–2009 recession and the attractiveness of Walmart's position as the dominant value player. But the jump in growth was twice the rate that analysts had expected, and according to the store's own analysis, it was fueled in particular by electronics products, the site of the greatest changes.[3]

In expanding your company, your choices are probably like Walmart's. If you are interested in growing in a way that fits your capabilities system and way to play, then there will be only four types of growth open to you:

1. You can grow the core of your business, getting more from your existing customers within the "headroom" of your current products and services, as Walmart did with its electronics department.

2. You can look for capability adjacencies. These are typically products and services that you haven't offered before and that allow you to apply your existing way to play and capabilities system in new market domains in ways that complement your existing offerings. Walmart accomplished this with its new offerings of pharmacies and fresh fruits and vegetables.

3. You can expand your geographic footprint, moving to new places where your capabilities system applies, as Walmart did successfully in the United Kingdom.

4. You can build new capabilities that expand (or replace) your existing way to play, potentially giving yourself a whole new platform for growth. This is by far the riskiest growth approach, and Walmart has tried here, too, with its neighborhood markets, which have about one-fourth the floor space of a regular Walmart store.

All four forms of growth can involve both organic "building" (through innovation, product launches, and business development) and inorganic "buying" (through mergers, acquisitions, partnerships, and alliances). The most effective companies may pursue both building and buying as the growth option requires. (We'll look at mergers and acquisitions in more detail in chapter 8.)

We show the four types of growth in a bull's-eye pattern (figure 7-1), because the approach that tends to generate the most value is the one at the center. Your options get progressively more expensive and riskier as you move toward the periphery.

The greatest value in growth comes from considering all of these options with a sense of coherence: recognizing explicitly how your way to play and capabilities system can make productive, profitable growth possible. Let's look at each in turn.

Headroom: Growth from the Core

We agree with *Profit from the Core* author Christopher Zook that your most promising growth strategy is to expand on your already strong core business.[4] Growing from the core should certainly be thoughtfully considered before other avenues of growth, which are all riskier. One

FIGURE 7-1

Four types of growth

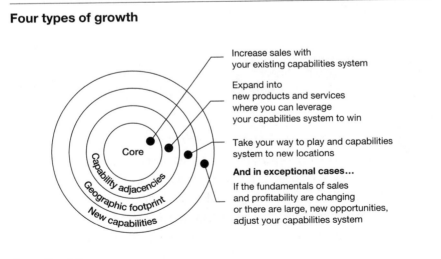

Source: Booz & Company.

thing you already know about your existing customer base is how well your way to play works with them. Growing within the core can also pave the way for other types of expansion. By building up the capabilities that you need for serving your existing customers more effectively, you may establish a level of coherence that can improve your chances elsewhere.

But we differ from Zook in our concept of the core. He sees it as your existing array of products and services. We argue, however, that if these are not coherent, then your growth efforts may be met with failure and lost investment.

It's telling that Walmart chose this route. It didn't revise its way to play or capabilities system. Its status as a supreme value player had served it well and was still defensible. Instead, its leaders made a deliberate effort to increase the chain's coherence. Then they looked for the hidden opportunities related to Walmart's existing way to play and capabilities.

Similarly, the most promising growth prospect for your company is likely to be the headroom in the markets where you are most coherent. *Headroom* is the maximum potential market share that a company can reasonably stand to gain. See the box "Estimating Your Headroom" to calculate what that market share might be.

Once you have estimated your headroom, or prospects for growth, ask why your current way to play is not reaching these prospects. Do

ESTIMATING YOUR HEADROOM

To estimate your headroom in a category, start by getting a clear sense of your way to play. Next, calculate the market share that you currently lack but that would respond to this way to play: the percentage of potential customers who are not buying your relevant products or services. Then subtract the market share you won't get: the percentage of customers who, for one reason or another, cannot switch to your offering or will never do so. The remainder represents your prospects for growth.

your customers not have access to you? Are your capabilities not developed or well integrated enough? Or is there simply another competitor that has executed a similar way to play more effectively?

Like Walmart, you almost certainly have more headroom in your existing core businesses than you expect. We are always surprised by how quick business leaders are to move beyond the core, when they presume that growth has run out there—and how much more growth is available there, once they return to look for it.

For many years, for example, Clorox managed its Kingsford charcoal briquettes like most of its other packaged goods, budgeting for a traditional mix of advertising, sales, supply chain, and R&D spending. The briquettes business was seen as a seasonal product, associated mostly with summertime.

In Kingsford, Clorox took on a way to play as an experience provider. It wasn't just selling a bag of charcoal fuel for cooking fires; it was supporting a family occasion with high emotional impact. This realization opened up new doors for the business, including extending the grilling season into the football season and up to Thanksgiving. The company also began developing partnerships with food brands (such as Johnsonville Sausage, Ballpark Franks (Sara Lee), Coca-Cola, Tyson, Clorox's own Hidden Valley Ranch, and Anheuser-Busch), with retailers, and with professional sports teams. Clorox's formidable merchandising and partnership capabilities were deployed to support the new approach; it positioned briquettes as the centerpiece of a larger impulse purchase (such as supplies for a "tailgate at home" autumn barbecue party). Some capabilities, such as traditional marketing or major new innovations, became less of a priority. As a result of these efforts, the Kingsford briquettes business soon became (and continues to be) one of the healthiest growth engines for the company. It also created valuable category for Clorox's retail partners.

Another example was Barclays Bank, which in 2003 discovered that many of its U.K. customers had a very narrow relationship with it. "Customers who thought of us as their bank," CEO John Varley later recalled, "often had only one or two accounts with us, and the rest with competitors." Barclays—like several other banks—discovered that there was headroom in the business of existing customers, if it was willing to develop its capabilities for customer engagement further. It turned out that many customers were interested in having their banking relationships all under one roof, especially if it could be done simply, and if there were incentives, like fee reductions, for switching. But under the current system, Barclay's made that difficult; every new account required separate paperwork, and the systems were not linked together.

The resulting efforts to improve the bank's back-office and customer management capabilities, spanning internal business unit boundaries to do so, led to a much improved lineup of integrated products and services. Under one new program called Open Plan, for instance, the bank gives a discount on mortgage interest for customers who have money held in Barclays savings and checking accounts. "The typical savings—about £700 per year for every £100,000 borrowed—reduces our margins," wrote Varley, "but it leads to a big increase in the number of products people hold." Customers could now also deal with one banker for every service Barclays offered.

To foster the improvement in its capabilities system, Barclays streamlined its organization, decentralizing operations so more decisions could be made locally. In support of this, Varley halved the size of the executive committee to five members.[5] That degree of internal change might seem excessive, but Varley and the bank's leaders recognized how essential it was to improve their capabilities. If Barclays had just launched the new products without improving its customer engagement and management, the initiative wouldn't have been successful. It would merely have cannibalized the margin on existing customers.

Capability Adjacencies: Avoiding the Adjacency Trap

There is no question that *adjacencies*—movement into new arenas related to your core business—can be incredibly successful. They should be considered part of your growth strategy. If you can apply your way to play and capabilities system in the new arena, the move will generally turn out to be successful. If not, it will either fail or require enormous (and probably incoherent) investment to succeed.

Unfortunately, many companies fall into the adjacency trap as they pursue this growth path. They extend their product lines, looking for untapped markets that seem close to their existing businesses, but they misjudge the capabilities they will need and assume that they themselves are naturally equipped to enter that new market.

Consider, for example, the no-frills second brands offered by several mainstream air carriers in the 1990s and 2000s. Most of these, including United Airlines' TED, Delta's Song, and Air Canada's Tango, failed. The parent carriers spent hundreds of millions of dollars on new branding, processes, and routes, but could never match the cost model of the original low-cost carriers such as Southwest Airlines and Ryanair. Arguably, the unsuccessful airlines might have made different decisions if they had looked more closely at the capabilities needed for running this different form of airline. The new brand required capabilities in employee management, marketing, operations, and ticket pricing that the incumbent airlines either wouldn't or couldn't bring to bear.

Perhaps the most compelling cautionary tale about the adjacency trap is the story of Anheuser-Busch in the 1980s. Its ill-fated effort to get into the snack food business seemed like a good idea to the company at the time. Beer and snack foods would seem to be natural adjacencies. They are consumed together, both rely on strong marketing and distribution, and both use yeast in production (at least for some snacks). Snack foods were an attractive adjacent market valued at $11 billion.[6] It had high growth and didn't appear at first glance to have huge barriers to entry. Anheuser-Busch was rolling in cash, having bested rival Miller Brewing Co. in the beer wars of the late 1970s.[7] The Anheuser-Busch value chain was already familiar with selling pretzels and snacks to bars and restaurants. How much of a problem could it be to expand that distribution to the snack food aisle of grocery stores and delis?

A closer look at the capabilities system needed to thrive in snack foods might have saved Anheuser-Busch from an enormously costly mistake. Beer and snack food have several capabilities in common—brand differentiation, consumer insight, distribution management, superior merchandising, and shelf management—but there are important differences, particularly in distribution and product innovation.

Alcohol distribution in the United States is a heavily regulated, state-based, three-tier system; fewer than three thousand distributors are licensed by one or more state governments to distribute beer. They get their product from licensed brewers and importers and sell only to licensed retailers. When Anheuser-Busch announced the Eagle Snacks launch, its independent beer distributors were either ill prepared or disenchanted. As one distributor told *BusinessWeek*, "We didn't want to dilute our focus. It may sound nice that beer and snacks go together, but not from a business standpoint."[8]

Indeed, distribution proved far more complicated and costly than Anheuser-Busch's executives had imagined. Snacks and beer have fundamentally different weight and volume characteristics. They are stocked in different parts of the typical grocery store (snacks at the end of the aisle, beer on refrigerated shelves), they often enter the store through different doors (snacks in front, beer at the back), and they are ordered by a different staff of buyers. Since the beer market is regulated, Anheuser-Busch was not used to snack-food aisle merchandising techniques and therefore ended up paying for shelf space, whereas Frito-Lay (with its direct-store delivery system) did not. These expenses further eroded Anheuser-Busch's margins, and the company never realized the hoped-for synergies between beer and snack distribution.[9] As for innovation, the two categories had vastly different product turnover rates. Snacks require constant change in flavor and packaging, while mainstream beer does not.

Furthermore, the beer maker had picked the wrong market to play in as an amateur. With no differentiated way to play, it was going up against the formidable direct-store delivery system of Frito-Lay, the King Kong of the snack food aisle—and a company with much more relative coherence. When Eagle Snacks started making incursions into Frito-Lay's snack stronghold in stores, the hammer came down. Frito-Lay mobilized its world-class capabilities system in direct-store delivery, consumer marketing, and innovation, launching an array of new products while upgrading distribution and slashing prices. Roger Enrico, who had just taken the reins at Frito-Lay, sent his ten thousand route drivers out to battle, instructing some to stay in the largest supermarkets full time to restock the shelves on a continual basis. He cut costs, initiating layoffs in some parts of the organization (these were the first layoffs in Frito-Lay's history) while simultaneously going on offense with investments in product quality. Eagle Snacks, with its cobbled-together distribution system and comparatively weak access to point-of-sale data, could not compete. Its share of market never topped 6 percent, while Frito-Lay's increased from 40 to 50 percent.[10]

Anheuser-Busch had launched Eagle Snacks in 1979. In 1995, after losing $25 million on sales of $400 million, it put Eagle Snacks on the block. No one made a serious bid for the business. The beer maker ultimately sold the Eagle Snacks brand name to P&G for a small sum.[11] The only other return Anheuser-Busch saw on its sixteen-year investment was a paltry $135 million on the "fire sale" of four of its plants— to none other than Frito-Lay. Ultimately, Anheuser-Busch wrote down the value of its Eagle Snacks investment, causing its shares to take a $500 million hit.[12]

The adjacency trap, which the airlines and Anheuser-Busch fell into, is all too common. The problem typically starts when a company expands into some seemingly congruent business, then discovers that its existing capabilities system is not adequate for success in that new market. Because it didn't prepare for this, it gets distracted catching up—either adding new capabilities it didn't plan for (which also adds to incoherence) or simply trying to marshal its resources more effectively. Meanwhile, there are inevitably entrenched competitors, like Southwest Airlines or Frito-Lay, with the necessary capabilities already at a formidable level of effectiveness and scale. The company that sought adjacencies becomes a second-place competitor, pouring an increasing amount of money into a capability that only supports a narrow piece of its business. By that time, it's too late to exit with any profitability—the only question is whether to take substantial losses now or even more substantial losses later. Worse, the capabilities that truly matter don't get the attention and investment they need, which creates openings for other competitors. This also happened to Anheuser-Busch: while their attention was diverted by snack foods, the Anheuser-Busch executives missed the emergent challenge of microbreweries.

To avoid the adjacency trap, you need to do more than just consider either the market potential or your capabilities in isolation. If your company is looking at expansion into an adjacent category, you should first look at your proposed way to play and your capabilities system in that context. How does this combination give you the right to win in this new market? What effect will this investment have on the rest of your company?

Two companies that have successfully managed audacious adjacency moves are Apple Computer, Inc., and Disney. As we saw in chapter 4,

Apple has parlayed a single capabilities system into a wide variety of seemingly unrelated sectors, and Disney's example is even more telling. The company's way to play has been much the same since Walt Disney first drew Mickey Mouse: to attract a particular audience through a variety of content channels, from film to television, theater, events, theme parks, and clothing retail (which Disney treats as a form of entertainment), with an emphasis on characters and drama. Who but Disney would have recognized that the capabilities needed to entertain a family in Orlando's Disney World could be adapted for *The Lion King* on Broadway?

The capabilities involved are highly sophisticated in content development, channel management, experience design, and copyright law; the Disney corporation has spent years building and applying them. It has a knack for taking something that others see as undifferentiated, like theme parks (in the 1950s) or computer animation (with its purchase of Pixar), and making it distinctively Disney's own. On occasions, when it makes a foray outside this way to play, as it does occasionally (for example, with its purchase of Miramax Studios), even Disney tends to fall into the adjacency trap.

A well-designed adjacency move brings a further benefit: it makes your capabilities system stronger and thus improves the prospects for your existing products and services. That's why we often suggest that companies seek to expand here first, rather than moving into new markets. Before making any adjacency move, ask yourself, will it make your whole enterprise stronger and add to your existing capabilities? Or will it drain resources from your existing capabilities system, without contributing back? If the answer is the latter, then it's probably a trap.

Expanding Your Geographic Footprint

Most companies trying to gain a foothold in new geographic areas don't necessarily think about the challenge in terms of their right to win. If it's an emerging market, they ask, "Don't we need to be in this market? Isn't this the place we're supposed to find growth?" If it's an established, mature market, they ask, "Don't we have to be here for the sake of our global brand presence?" Then they worry about barriers to entry, like regulations and the privileged relationships that competitors based in those countries enjoy. They end up with incoherent operations, with multiple ways to play and capabilities systems around the world, and comparatively poor return on their investment.

When considering a market, start by asking about the basis of your ability to win there. If the answer has to do with the strength of your capabilities system, but you must append it with some table-stakes capabilities to compete, then it is certainly worth considering. If, however, your capabilities system does not apply, or it doesn't include the critical capabilities that are necessary to win, then entry will be much more challenging. The most effective option is usually to enter countries that are part of a geographic cluster—a group of countries with similar or complementary attributes, such as socioeconomic profile, infrastructure, language, or market dynamics—where you can master a capabilities system that can give you the right to win in many of those countries.

Several telecommunications companies, such as Vodafone (Germany), Telenor (Norway), MTN (South Africa), Etisalat (United Arab Emirates), and Saudi Telecom (Saudi Arabia), have deployed, in effect, a two-stage process for entering countries in Africa, Asia, and the broader Middle East. It started when the telecom companies realized that their familiar way to play and capabilities system would not apply in high-growth emerging markets (like Afghanistan, Bangladesh, India, Indonesia, Nigeria, Sri Lanka, and Tanzania). People in these countries avidly want mobile phones, traditional (fixed-line) telecom systems are rare, and disposable income is very limited compared to more mature markets. What's more, the telecom foreigners compete against local companies that have a strong understanding of the consumers and business practices of their home markets. Thus, the foreign new entrants had to adopt a differentiated approach in these markets—coming in from the outside to compete with the innovation and fast-follower strengths that they brought with them.

However, they also had to master the new capabilities systems required for the new markets they entered. Thus, in the first stage—with the economy still very much in an emerging state—they developed new capabilities around lean operations, low-cost business models (in part through aggressive infrastructure sharing and indirect distribution channels), and innovation tailored to low income users. These were quite different from their strengths in home markets; indeed, some of the innovations they developed, such as mobile-phone-based payment systems for people without bank accounts, were often banned in their home countries but highly relevant in these new markets. At the same time, the entering phone companies could play to a strength that only they had: they understood how the telecom market looked when it matured, and therefore they could anticipate products and services that would be needed in the future.

During the first stage, the telecom companies essentially maintained two ways to play and capabilities systems—one for new markets and one for their older, mature home countries. But now, as some of the emerging economies enter a second stage of development, the two capabilities systems are starting to complement each other. For example, several multi-region telecommunications companies are transferring their newly developed operating models (with lean operations and low-cost set-ups) back to their home markets. This allows them to reduce expenses, and thereby make pricing more competitive. Some are applying their mobile-phone payment innovations back in Europe as micropayment systems for news and entertainment media.

Building New Capabilities

What about growth pursued outside the core—with new businesses that require so many new capabilities that you must, in effect, create an altogether new company and change your way to play? Frankly, we are skeptical of most of these opportunities. A strategy based on this option is the most difficult to pull off. Moreover, blue-ocean-inspired efforts to grow outside the core can distract you from the opportunities in the headroom right in front of you, where you already have a right to win.[13]

Nonetheless, there are times when you face a choice about your company: either reinvent it from scratch or seek to sell your business to someone who will. The two triggers for this are generally major technological or political changes. For example, a new kind of device comes along that provides a challenge and an opportunity, or a government that has protected you now seeks to privatize your company.

One of the great cautionary business tales is the way that Polaroid, the creator of instant photography, fell prey to the rise of digital photography. At first glance, this might seem like an argument against coherence, because nobody ever accused the company's founder and CEO, Edwin H. Land, of being incoherent. As a former research engineer who started his career at Polaroid has put it to us, a little indelicately, "Land was coherent, all the way to oblivion."

But on closer examination, it's clear that Polaroid was not held back by its way to play or capabilities, but on the way it defined itself. The company acted as if its crown jewel were the instant-camera technology, rather than the capabilities it had built up in creating and marketing that technology. One symptom of this was the company's failure to commercialize some of its other technologies invented in its labs, such as flat batteries and miniature motors. The company's way to play—as an innovator of technology and components—could have naturally fit a digital world; marketing instant pictures on emulsion could have evolved easily into marketing images stored on computer chips. Polaroid could have also looked for businesses where these innovation capabilities could have thrived—for example, in other personal electronics. But it did not, or could not, marshal those capabilities for any other project. In 2001—ten years after Land died—Polaroid, overrun by the revolution in digital photography, filed for bankruptcy protection. Today, all that remains of Polaroid's once glorious history is its brand name.

By contrast, consider the nineteenth-century example—described by business historian Randall Stross—of the successful shift of a few horse-drawn carriage makers, such as Studebaker and Timken, to making automobiles.[14] Because they had a way to play built around personal transportation vehicles, these businesses recognized that their capabilities applied to this new, seemingly unfamiliar technology. In an age of horseless carriages, people would still need seats, doors, wheel springs for a relatively comfortable ride, and other amenities. The shift by Pitney Bowes from leasing postage meters to communications-related software and services (such as validating addresses for call centers) and International Data Group's transition from publishing magazines about computers in print to creating comprehensive online media environments are two more recent examples.[15]

Organic and Inorganic Growth

Three further lessons apply to your growth strategy in general. First, there will always be a reason to look for growth. Opportunities will emerge, and market dynamics may change. Even the most coherent company must avoid complacency and continue to scan its environment.

Second, define your growth plans by what you do, not by what you have. Capabilities are more flexible than assets. When you need to expand to new customers, markets, geographies, or entirely new ways to play, you will be able to do so without having to reinvent your entire organization.

Third, integrate mergers and acquisitions as part of your overall growth plan. Building out your business through marketing and R&D will probably be insufficient. If your way to play involves maintaining above-average returns, some form of inorganic growth may well be necessary.[16] M&A must therefore be evaluated as part of a coherent company's growth strategy. In the next chapter, we'll look at this subject in more detail.

CHAPTER EIGHT

MERGERS AND ACQUISITIONS

Why did Amazon buy Zappos, the online shoe and apparel store, in 2009? It wasn't primarily for the shoes; Amazon already owned a shoe site called Endless.com. It wasn't primarily for the existing Zappos Web interface—Endless's interface was at least as attractive—or the cash flow. Zappos was a ten-year-old company with a loyal following, but it was barely profitable.

The acquisition wasn't really for assets at all. It was for the capabilities—and, in particular, for the contribution Zappos would make to Amazon's own capabilities system. The Zappos case is a clear example of the main point of this chapter: the companies that create the most value combine organic growth with mergers and acquisitions (M&A), all in the service of developing and expanding a capabilities system.

Zappos had capabilities in retail interface design and customer-relationship management that, on the surface, seemed close to Amazon's own. But Zappos, largely through ingenuity and its own creative culture, had outpaced the larger retailer. Amazon was known for its automated approach to customer service, in which human intermediaries were almost never needed—but if you did need one, it was impossible to find a phone number to talk with them. Zappos, by contrast, put its toll-free number on every page, encouraged customers to call it, and staffed and trained its call center representatives to cultivate shoppers' interest. Customer service was so important to the company that it moved its headquarters from San Francisco to Las Vegas to take advantage of the latter city's well-trained customer service workforce (from the hospitality industry), twenty-four-hour culture, and lower cost of living. Similarly, Zappos maintained a presence on social media networks like Twitter; if you sent a tweet praising a shoe you had bought, a Zappos staff member would typically respond within thirty minutes—a compelling institutional response for a social-media aficionado.

Though Amazon had reason to keep its approach to customer service intact, founder Jeff Bezos recognized that the Zappos approach produced extremely high rates of customer satisfaction, even compared with Amazon's. Moreover, in buying Zappos, Bezos was absorbing a competitor that, like Amazon itself, was focused on the long term—and whose capabilities might help Amazon attract customers and better penetrate new markets. Gaining those capabilities and eliminating a potential source of long-term competition all in one fell swoop was too good an opportunity to pass up.

Amazon has a history of such purchases. It acquired Audible.com, which produces audiobooks—and which helped Amazon create a digital audio-reading feature for the Kindle. Amazon also acquired Joyo.com, the number one online bookstore in China, which helped the U.S. company build capabilities for logistics, distribution, and processing payments in China. After buying Digital Photography Review (dpreview.com), a digital-photography review Web site, Amazon became the world's richest forum of user-generated commentary on phones, PDAs, and computer-based devices. Its acquisition of the used-book information site Abe Books allowed it to solidify its position in the used, rare, and out-of-print book business and expand its network of affiliated book dealers.

In short, in its first fifteen years as an e-commerce pioneer, Amazon has systematically sought deals that bring it either complementary capabilities that fit its system, new arenas in which to use its capabilities more effectively, or both. You can do the same.

The Anatomy of Acquisitions

Not all acquisitions add value, but if you want to add value through a capabilities-driven strategy, then you need to consider M&A as part of your plan. When conducted with a capabilities-driven perspective, M&A deals are managed differently from conventional practice. During your research, for instance, besides evaluating the financials and growth opportunities, you'll have questions about coherence. Will the new company draw on your existing capabilities? Will it improve or strengthen what you already do? Or will it force you to invest in a new system of capabilities that you don't have any competence in right now? If some businesses coming in as part of this deal don't fit your capabilities system, how rapidly will you be able to sell them, at a good price, to a buyer who can make better use of them? In short, the coherent company looks to its acquisitions to support its existing strategy—not to start an entirely new strategic approach.

A growing body of empirical evidence supports the importance of coherence in M&A. One pair of studies examined the results of M&A deals in the U.S. health-care and utilities industries between 1995 and 2009. There were three types of acquisitions identified in the research:

Capability building: One group of acquisitions was focused on acquiring companies because they brought a needed new or better capability to support a primary way to play. For example, some health insurance companies purchased wellness and disease management firms so they could offer prevention services; others bought competitors with particularly good cost management or information technology capabilities.

Scale and consolidation: Another group aimed at purchasing other companies with the same basic types of product lines and capabilities, thereby using existing capabilities. For example, Boston Scientific acquired Guidant, a longtime competitor in the field of medical product manufacturing.

Diversification: The third group of deals was done to allow the acquiring company to enter a new sector or industry—either as a hedge against keeping all its business in one sector, or to chase attractive sectors (and therefore improve operating margins or growth), or to gain the presumed benefits of increased scale. These deals were often incoherent, because there was no reason for the new acquisitions to fit or improve the existing capabilities system.[1]

The health-care study found that the first two types of deals, as a whole, were significantly more successful than deals done with an eye to diversification. Deals done to add capabilities had 38 percent more winners than losers, as measured by the acquirers' stock prices one year out. Deals done for scale and consolidation purposes had an equal number of winners and losers, and deals done for the purpose of diversification (which would tend toward greater incoherence) were 40 percent more likely to fail than succeed.

The other study, of the utilities industry, yielded similar results. In both studies, the majority of deals done primarily for diversification tended not to work. The expected performance gains (often driven only by cost synergies) were undermined by the incoherence created from businesses that require distinct capabilities systems.

Acquiring for Growth

In deciding which deals represent the highest priority for your company, consider the same four types of growth described in chapter 7:

1. You can grow the core of your business, making acquisitions that allow you to deploy your capabilities system more effectively, as Amazon is doing by incorporating the customer-service aspects of Zappos.

2. You can look for capability adjacencies, buying new products and services where your way to play and capabilities system will apply, as Amazon did in buying Abe Books.

3. You can expand your geographic footprint, extending your existing capabilities system and offerings to new places and new customers, as Amazon did with Joyo.com in China. Even when a company's capabilities system applies in a new geographic area, there will always be unfamiliar elements of the business—particularly around

distribution, understanding customer requirements, legal issues, and regulatory management. For this reason, M&A deals (including alliances and partnerships) tend to be effective ways to enter new markets.[2]

4. You can acquire new capabilities and positions that expand (or replace) your existing way to play, potentially giving yourself a whole new platform for growth. Consider this type of deal only when you must shift to a new way to play—and when there is a credible path, through this deal, to creating a right to win for the new business.

As with organic growth, start where success is most assured—aligned to your capabilities system. Avoid the adjacency trap. It is all too easy to acquire companies that seem to have similar products or to move into a new geographic territory through acquisition, only to discover that the new companies or localities require vastly different capabilities to manage. Occupying the same category does not guarantee that the two businesses will mesh well, as many corporate leaders in (for example) the airlines or automotive industries could tell you.

In some cases, you can lower the risks and raise the value of M&A by taking advantage of your capabilities system: buying assets and capabilities that have been dumped at a discount by other companies, but that would work better for you than for competitors. Gradually, as businesses are sold to companies with more appropriate capabilities systems, a whole industry can evolve to become more coherent.

Growing Through M&A: Itaú Unibanco

Itaú Unibanco is an example of a company that understands how to grow through mergers and acquisitions—and how to use M&A to become a larger and more successful organization while maintaining coherence. This bank, which was created in 2008 through the merger of Banco Itaú and Unibanco, is the largest privately held financial services company in the Southern Hemisphere.

The bank has two main streams of corporate history.[3] The first dates back to 1924, when the bank Casa Moreira Salles was founded in southeastern Brazil. Later renamed Unibanco, it became one of the largest banks in the country after the 1995 acquisition of another Brazilian bank, Banco Nacional. The other stream of Itaú Unibanco's history started in 1945, when Banco Central de Crédito, later renamed Banco Itaú, was founded in São Paolo. Since then, this company acquired or merged with more than twenty banks in Latin America and forged alliances with many others.

Throughout their separate histories, both banks favored acquisitions that would mesh with their ways to play—which, as it happened, were fairly similar. During the 1980s and 1990s, both Itaú and Unibanco developed strategic identities as solutions providers for their clients: helping them navigate the inflationary, volatile economies of Brazil and the rest of Latin America. Then came the 2000s: both banks provided guidance as Brazil's economy shifted to greater stability, lower inflation, and the expectations of steady economic growth.

In November 2008, at the height of the global financial crisis, Unibanco and Itaú merged. Since then, with Brazil's financial influence growing worldwide, the quality and breadth of financial services in the country has become more important than ever, and the value of a solutions provider in banking is paramount. Itaú Unibanco's current strategy is to develop this way to play further, consolidating a host of financial services—that it has gained and continues to gain through acquisitions—into a relatively seamless group, adding scope without adding much complexity, and expanding into new locations in Latin America.

The bank executes this strategy with a distinctive capabilities system. One capability is related to openness and local customer engagement: when entering new markets, both in Brazil and then in other countries, Itaú Unibanco consistently demonstrates an understanding of local regulations and customers' needs. This is manifest in the bank's modest, self-effacing culture. Its executives acknowledge that they learned the importance of this from being on the other side of the equation: seeing foreign banks come into Brazil, ignore local conditions and limits, and fail to gain a footing.

The bank also distinguishes itself through first-rate operational capabilities, including its back-office processes and technologies, which it invested in earlier than most other Latin American banks. It is known for its *process discipline* in retail banking in particular: standardizing its processes and managing them seamlessly and rigorously across a wide variety of services. Unlike some other banks, it applies this discipline in its investment banking and private banking arms as well. "They are predictable and reliable," says one observer of the industry there. "Being their client is like eating at McDonald's: you might wish for different food at times, but you know what to expect."

A third capability has to do with understanding and working with local regulations, both in Brazil and elsewhere. For example, when Brazil began to privatize banks in the mid-1990s, Itaú was a major participant in the restructuring of the banking system. Itaú Unibanco has deployed this capability globally to gain a distinctive global presence in retail banking in Argentina, Chile, and Portugal and private banking in Luxembourg.

Together, these capabilities combine to create a reliable, multifaceted financial services operation. The capabilities system also helps Itaú Unibanco execute its M&A deals more effectively while maintaining its coherence afterward. In an acquisition, the value of the new entrant's processes, knowledge, products, and services largely depends on how well they fit with those of the acquirer. Concluding the financial part of the deal is no guarantee that they will fit. With its disciplined operations and understated approach to convening other organizations, Itaú Unibanco tends to find the process of absorbing other companies to be relatively easy and natural.

A Guide to Coherent M&A

Two practices deserve particular attention in making sure that deals yield value. These are the due diligence at the beginning and the postmerger integration at the end. Every company has its own way of handling both of these practices, and our intention here isn't to be comprehensive. But a few guidelines can help companies adjust those practices for a greater level of coherence.

First, when you conduct due diligence, do so with an eye toward capabilities. Successful M&A deals, conducted with a capabilities perspective, require stress tests that go beyond ordinary due diligence, which tends to focus mostly on financial and legal validity. Specifically, how applicable are the capabilities of the incoming company, and how well suited are its products and services to the capabilities system and way to play of the acquirer?

Second, emphasize postmerger integration even more than you otherwise might. The fit between the capabilities of the two companies, and their products and services, is critical to the success of the new enterprise. But it tends to be invisible in the deal, while the assets—the plants, customer list, and patents—show up more readily. Then, after the deal is consummated, investment in capabilities is often cut back further, to help justify the price that the acquirer has paid. Ironically, just when the right capabilities are needed the most, the pressure is highest to reduce them.

To avoid this, you should identify in advance the capabilities that should be preserved. Plan to migrate those and invest in the related parts of the business, while other parts of the business can be de-emphasized, closed, or sold. It's particularly important to retain the people who are critical in building or overseeing the capabilities you are acquiring.

The people negotiating the deal may not know which people and processes to focus attention on and which they can let go. As a smart business leader, you must therefore take steps to retain the people and capabilities that prompted your company to make the deal in the first place. You can do this through knowledge-oriented "SWAT teams" dedicated to integrating the two capabilities systems. When P&G bought Tambrands (the makers of Tampax) in 1997 and moved the incoming company's headquarters, the business leaders were very concerned that some employees might not stay. The company would therefore lose much of its tacit knowledge about the success of the brand, the capabilities related to the product, and the close consumer relationships that the company had fostered. So P&G interviewed many of the Tambrands veterans and made the transcripts searchable with fuzzy logic. Of course, this is not the only way to preserve the capabilities you are acquiring; whatever tactics you choose, it's important to plan for preserving not just the assets you acquire, but the capabilities as well.

Third, structure the new entity to foster coherence. Typically, integration means absorbing the incoming company or leaving it as a stand-alone entity. But it may be more effective to do what Mars did in

2008, when it acquired the Wm. Wrigley Jr. Company. Both Wrigley and Mars were remarkably focused, family-owned companies with strong confectionery businesses. Wrigley sold gum, mints (Altoids), hard candy (Lifesavers), and Eclipse breath strips. Mars had iconic brands in chocolate (M&M's, Milky Way, Snickers) and non-chocolate (Skittles, Starburst) candy. When Mars swept in with a $23 billion all-cash offer for Wrigley, the combination made so much sense that investing sage Warren Buffett committed $4.4 billion of the purchase price and a further $2.1 billion to purchase a stake in the Wrigley division. After two weeks of negotiation, Wrigley agreed.[4]

The executives at Mars then made a noteworthy decision; they left Wrigley as a stand-alone business, with its headquarters remaining in Chicago. They transferred their own non-chocolate brands, such as Starburst and Skittles, to Wrigley's portfolio. This provided the real underlying value in the acquisition: to create a new division for non-chocolate brands, with a way to play as a purveyor of innovative, flavored impulse purchases, and a capabilities system that would draw on both legacy enterprises and aim for relative coherence. Mars CEO Paul Michaels summed up the deal: "[It's] not about being bigger—it's about being the best."[5]

Finally, design the cost-cutting aspects of your M&A process with an eye toward coherence. Many acquisitions are justified by the promise of cost synergies; you assume, going into the deal, that redundant overhead will be cut. To maintain these synergies, your cost-cutting efforts should be based less on redundancy and more on a capabilities-oriented fit. Focus on selling businesses and downsizing functions that do not contribute to your way to play; this could be one of your greatest levers for capturing synergies without constraining the new organization's ability to win.

In the next chapter, on cutting costs, we'll look at this approach more broadly and show how a coherent company learns to stand behind its investment.

CHAPTER NINE

CUT COSTS AND GROW STRONGER

If you are like most executives, you have spent a lot of time thinking about costs. The pressure to reduce expenses—whether this pressure is driven by your cash flow, your shareholders, your uncertainty, or your investment needs—is always present. Frugality, productivity, and efficiency—the need to do more with less—are on every business agenda and have been scrutinized more intensely than ever since the economic crisis of 2008–2009.

But cost-cutting is typically practiced in a way that makes companies weaker and more limited, and most businesspeople assume that this is a necessary part of the exercise. We reject—and you should emphatically reject—this idea. If managed correctly, cost reduction should lead to better performance, making the company stronger by eliminating wasted expense. If you focus on strengthening your way to play and capabilities system, cutting costs can be a catalyst for exactly the change you need.

Costs and strategy are inseparable because every investment, whether good or bad, matters. Unnecessary cost is your enemy—and not just because it consumes profit. It is your enemy because it fuels incoherence.

It reinforces multiple activities that prevent you from focusing on your capabilities system and way to play.

In a relatively coherent company, the following conditions hold true:

- No strategy exercise is complete without a strong look at costs.

- No cost project is complete without a look at strategy.

- No cost *or* strategy project is complete without a clear look at its impact on the company's capabilities system.

- All cost-cutting is seen as the way to free up the investments you need most.

Finally, your approach to cost control is a key indicator of how coherent your company is (or is not). If you haven't freed up resources to invest in the capabilities you need most, then you haven't gone far enough on the journey to coherence. That's because you're never just cutting costs; you're deciding that some things are more strategically relevant than others.

Cost-Cutting and Its Discontents

Why do conventional approaches to cutting costs leave companies weaker? The answer has to do with ingrained incoherence. Without a clear way to play or a capabilities system to guide priorities, leaders focus mechanically and programmatically on reducing the pain of cost-cutting. For this reason, they cut across the board, instituting, say, a 10 percent workforce reduction to be shared by all departments. They make cuts based on ad hoc, sometimes even capricious, criteria. They benchmark the cost levels of competitors, without comparing their own strategic priorities—which means, in effect, that the leaders base their decisions on the mistakes of other companies or on their competitors' strategies. Or they relegate the problem to special initiatives: a yearly cost analysis or a biannual audit of SG&A (selling, general, and administrative) expenses. The recommendations are overlaid on top of everyday operations and seen, in effect, as a constraint that the organization must endure.

The result of all this? The cutbacks generate a great deal of pain in the short term. Then when good times roll again, companies revert to their old habits as if nothing was learned. After all, the old forms of incoherence—the overinvestment for the sake of matching competitors, the desire to be excellent in all things, the proliferation of growth activities, the continual focus on putting out fires—have never gone away. Marketing gets its budget replaced (at least in part), R&D and manufacturing get theirs, M&A proposals are considered again, and so on down the line. Worse yet, while the budgets of some functions and divisions may not return to normal, these groups continue to be asked to deliver the same level of service and complexity. So they struggle even more in the new, post-recovery environment.

Sometimes this leads to a second round of haphazard, ad hoc layoffs and cost reductions—and then to a third and fourth. Cutbacks that come in waves produce further problems. In one January 2009 survey of U.S. corporate executives, 72 percent said they expected to make across-the-board cuts. They knew that doing this would hurt their top-line revenue streams, but they felt they had no choice.[1]

Ultimately, the leaders of these companies find themselves in the same position that three high-ranking executives we know found themselves in. Each of them came to us in late 2009 or early 2010 with the same complaint: "We can't figure it out. We took out all these costs eighteen months ago, and now they're back."

The Conversation About Costs

To take expenses out of your system and keep them out, you need to change your conversation about costs to a more productive one. Part of your existing conversation is probably about blame. In many companies, because functions contain most of the "cost centers" of the enterprise, functional leaders tend to be held responsible—implicitly or explicitly—for creating bloated cost structures. Is this fair? Occasionally. But more often than not, functional leaders are guilty of nothing more than responding to the incoherent strategy of the moment.

Let's say that the head of information technology at one company has been given a long list of projects to fulfill: virtualization, customer-relationship management, cloud computing, and service-oriented architecture, each for a different part of the business. The operations chief must accommodate twelve new product lines. The R&D leader is figuring out which investments to fund, without a clear mandate to guide the choice. Even the CFO is spending in an ad hoc fashion, exploring a series of unrelated acquisitions.

In this company, no one considers which functional endeavors are most essential to the company's advantage. No one, especially none of the functional leaders, is given the right to say no to any requests. But when the costs are all added up, these leaders will be at least partly blamed for it.

Another part of the existing conversation has to do with control. When cutbacks take place without an obvious and clear strategy, you as a business unit leader or line manager feel as if someone from above has taken the autonomy away from your business. Decisions made from outside can seem arbitrary; they inevitably force you to renege on some promises or kill some projects that are already showing potential.

If you expect to promote coherence in your company, you need to change these conversations up front. Convert them into the kind of conversation you should have had all along: about the value of your endeavors. "A Process for Cutting Costs" shows an exercise that can accomplish this.

A PROCESS FOR CUTTING COSTS

Purpose: To set in place a plan to cut costs while your company grows stronger, particularly if you're in a hurry. This process assumes that you have an idea of your way to play and capabilities system; it is most effectively used in the transformation step of a capabilities-driven strategy.

Process: In what might be several days of conversation (plus associated research, if needed), you and the rest of the executive team need to look at the expense sheet with a fresh eye and an imaginary parking lot.

Start by dividing your costs into four basic groups:

1. **Lights on:** The bare minimum expenses to keep the business going fall into this category. These include money spent on facilities, bare-bones legal work, the most unavoidable operational expenses, and precious little else. These costs probably represent 10 to 20 percent of your total expenses.

2. **Table stakes:** These are the expenses that you must pay to maintain your position in your industry, even though your business might run without them. These might include customer-relationship systems or even some very basic forms of product improvement. Be sure to distinguish the true table stakes from nonessential customer-related expenses. This category typically represents no more than 20 to 30 percent of the total; it's in your interest to make it as small as possible in your exercise.

3. **Capabilities-driven costs:** These involve the costs that support your capabilities system and way to play. Most of these should be funded in good times and bad. They may deserve more resources than you are currently allotting them. This could add up to as much as 20 to 30 percent of the total.

4. **Everything else:** All expenses that do not specifically fit into the first three categories are included here. The list should be long; it may include parts of the customer care, information technology, sales, and logistics departments. It may include whole functions. But if the company could keep running without them and if they are not part of your capabilities system, they belong in this group. The exercise, if conducted dispassionately, will probably relegate at least 30 percent, and perhaps 50 percent or more, of your costs to this group.

For the moment, put aside the first three categories. List everything in the fourth category—your discretionary expenses—on a whiteboard, as if you were moving them all out to a metaphorical parking lot. Remember, these are your optional, or discretionary, expenses. Calculate how much money your company would save annually (or have available to reinvest) if you simply cut these expenses entirely. All of them. This may sound hard-hearted and perhaps counterproductive. But we are still operating in the safe environment of the exercise.

Now it is time to get real. One by one, move the expenses that you think should be saved back into the metaphorical building. The ones you are moving back represent those you are deciding to keep. Each represents a different bet, large or small, on some aspect of the future of your business.

As you talk through the possibilities, consider the trade-offs and risks for each item: the downside that the business would face if it made the cuts and changes you are considering. Going through the list could take some time, but when you are done, your groups will now have evolved into five:

1. Lights-on expenses

2. Table-stakes expenses

3. The expenses you moved back from the parking lot

4. The expenses still out there in the lot

5. The expenses related to your capabilities system

Combine the first three items in the preceding list: the lights-on expenses, the table-stakes expenses, and the expenses you moved back from the parking lot. Although you have decided to keep these expenses, they do not differentiate your company. Take another look at them, this time with an eye toward increasing efficiency or lowering service levels. Look for opportunities to increase their efficiency, to outsource them, or to recalibrate them toward lower cost levels, perhaps giving up the best-in-class status of some of them. How frugal can you be with these and still get the value you need?

Also examine at the investments required to bring your capabilities system up to speed. Anything you spend on this will have to come from activities you leave out in the parking lot—and it will make the decisions that much harder. How would you justify further investment in these? How can you maximize the value you receive? What other activities would have to be cut—or eliminated—to fulfill the needs of your capabilities system?

Now look at the expenses still out in the parking lot. You have decided, in effect, that these are expendable. In the short term, you may have to continue to support these aspects of your business, but this shouldn't prevent an open discussion about their long-term fate. Be explicit about the costs that would come out of the system if you sold or discontinued them, versus the benefits that would accrue from keeping them.

Challenge the need to keep these investments at all. Many costs undoubtedly relate to pieces of your business that operate at cross-purposes with your strategy. Ask yourself how your overall cost allocations would change if these businesses were no longer part of the portfolio. While you may not decide (or be able) to sell them in the short term, this will give you a better idea of how your costs have been generated. (You can also use the portfolio matrix in figure 6-1 to help evaluate these businesses.) As with the rest of this exercise, your ultimate objective is to see all of your expenses as additive—as consciously chosen, rather than merely accepted because they are legacy expenses.

The Opportunity of a Crisis

Some of the most significant and successful moves toward coherence occur when management realizes, "If we don't turn ourselves around, we may not survive." These urgent situations provide an impetus to make critical strategic changes, including the reinvention of the company's way to play and capabilities system. In other words, a crisis can provide a chance to reorient your company to a new business environment—if you seize the opportunity.

In the early 1990s, this type of challenge faced the automobile battery division of Johnson Controls, Inc. (JCI). (The car-seat division of the same company was featured in chapter 3.) The retailer Sears, Roebuck and Co., which represented 20 percent of JCI's business in motor vehicle batteries, suddenly pulled its contract. The reasons had nothing to do with JCI's products or service, but the company nonetheless faced huge overcapacity and steep losses, almost overnight. JCI's top executives reacted by looking at their business with fresh eyes.

To make the new approach work, JCI built up its prowess in lean manufacturing, six sigma, and operational flexibility. In the past, production had been organized to get the highest performance out of every individual assembly line, with many plants devoted to particular models. Now JCI's executives looked at operations as a single network, reconfiguring production flows as needed to serve customers more flexibly. They treated the cost of shipping batteries—which had been a primary factor in their previous configurations—as just one of the many variables to consider, and they explicitly redesigned the flow to reduce complexity. This reduced the costs they had to manage. They also identified other cuts in areas where their capabilities were not differentiated, such as accounting, human resources, and information technology. Altogether, they cut about $150 million annually, which at the time represented about 35 percent of their expenses. They understood that they might make some mistakes in implementing those cuts, but they knew that they had to act decisively and fix any errors later.

By the fourth quarter of 1995, despite the loss of revenues, profits had began to rise again.[2] In later years, when executives looked back on this crisis, they thought of it as a moment of transformation for Johnson Controls and an example to emulate. By engaging in a high-level strategic analysis and then converting their conclusions into action, they had turned their company around. Other observers agreed; for example, an analyst's report from that time on "hot stocks" recommended investing in JCI, because the "repositioning and restructuring of the [battery] business . . . looks like a modern business miracle."[3]

In the long run, this shift laid a foundation for still-stronger logistics, global marketing, and innovation capabilities. Today, JCI sells automobile batteries internationally under such brand names as LTH (Mexico), Varta (Europe and China), and Optima. It has been a leader in developing IT-enhanced warehousing and logistics capabilities for reducing costs and increasing market intelligence for auto component retailers. JCI has also become a leading battery design innovator. Selling increasingly to auto manufacturers, it has developed new technologies for microhybrid (diesel-electric) vehicles, which require battery chemistries that can handle frequent stops and starts. The company is perhaps unique in producing both traditional (lead-acid) batteries and new lithium-ion batteries for electric and hybrid vehicles. In short, a challenge that could have led to retrenchment and incoherence became, instead, the beginning of a twenty-year-long transformation to a customer-focused, innovative company that is unusually well prepared, compared to the rest of their industry, for whatever powertrain technologies become dominant in the next few years.

Another example of adapting to turbulent change by embracing coherence took place with the R.J. Reynolds Tobacco Company in the early 2000s—as a response to a complete shift in the industry structure over a few years. R.J. Reynolds had spent the previous thirty years as, essentially, an experience provider: cigarettes, before their negative health effects became publicized, were primarily marketed for the smoking experience and the statement they projected about the individual. (Camel smokers were fun-loving; Marlboro smokers were rugged; Dunhill's smokers were high-class.) The margins on a cigarette pack were high enough that an individual smoker's brand loyalty was worth a great deal for a tobacco company, and tobacco companies spent generously on marketing to win that loyalty. In the 1950s and 1960s, they had done this through mass-market brand advertising. Then after 1971, when they were forbidden from advertising on television in the United States, they built up a new capabilities system, aimed at winning the "war in the store" for customers. This included sophisticated promotions: using coupons, premiums (gifts for buying a small number of cartons), and in-store displays to persuade smokers to try their brand. At one point, competition through premiums was so intense that R.J. Reynolds became the largest purchaser of T-shirts in the United States. Another capability was embedded in its elaborate sales force: securing shelf space, maintaining the racks, and moving premiums and promotions into and out of particular sales outlets whenever the competition heated up. The cigarette companies paid for all this by raising prices when they needed to.

Then came the U.S. government's 1998 Tobacco Master Settlement Agreement, ratified by the four largest U.S. tobacco companies (R.J. Reynolds, Philip Morris, Brown & Williamson, and Lorillard) and the attorneys general of forty-six states. The agreement required the cigarette companies to pay out about $206 billion to the states over twenty-five years, in return for settling the case. Since only the major cigarette makers had to pay these damages at first (the agreement was later expanded to others), the opportunity rapidly arose for new, low-cost tobacco manufacturers to enter the market with so-called value brands. This forced cigarette prices lower, cutting back the major cigarette companies' top lines at the moment that the first payments to the states hit their bottom lines, in a declining market, with fewer and fewer new smokers every year.

Whatever your view of the tobacco industry, there is no denying the impact of a declining market on tobacco companies—or the imperative it gave them to find a new approach to their business. To start with, the executives at R.J. Reynolds realized that their old capabilities system—geared to support and promote the market-share-gaining brand Camel and the profitable but shrinking brands Winston and Salem—was no longer sustainable. Nor would cutting costs, in itself, solve the problem unless they could change the way they went to market and the tools they used. They needed a fundamentally new way to play with a fully new capabilities system.

Simply to survive, they initiated a major short-term cost-cutting program, including laying off a large portion of the workforce. But RJR's leaders did not make cuts across the board or try to compete as a value player. Instead, they focused on becoming an experience provider in a narrower domain. They continued to support Camel aggressively, while dramatically cutting back support for RJR's other brands, Winston and Salem. And they looked at the value that R.J. Reynolds could gain by changing its merchandising capabilities.

In particular, they moved rapidly away from full-scale, in-store marketing to a new "sharp-pencil" (targeted) marketing capability. There would be no more T-shirts and ball caps (and sourcing them would no longer be a critical capability). The arrival of an R.J. Reynolds salesperson at a retail shop would no longer mean a check for the shopkeeper with the notation "promotional support" on it. R.J. Reynolds would cut down its sales force, negotiate space more strictly, "buy" shelf space with promotions (featuring selected retail stores) instead of with cash, and build its relationships with those key store owners.

It was a strategic leap—and a huge risk. R.J. Reynolds was betting that it could re-create a new, slimmed-down sales force that could change the nature of the conversation at the point of sale. Executives deliberated over the likely response: would retailers still welcome their reps? How would the company build brand loyalty now?

In the end, it worked; R.J. Reynolds gained $1 billion in cost reductions. The company's bottom line improved, which gave it the controlling position in its merger with Brown and Williamson a short time later. As the benefits of its strategy became increasingly evident, R.J. Reynolds stock rose threefold over a twenty-two-month period, putting it in the top fifteen *Fortune* 500 companies, measured by returns.[4]

In the case of both JCI and R.J. Reynolds, the key to the change was *not* cutting costs in itself. Through the creative energy released in the crisis, company leaders decided on a way to play and a capabilities system—and therefore ensured that some costs would be worthwhile, while others could be jettisoned.

If you find yourself in a similar situation, you will need to bring the same creative energy to bear, perhaps to make a change of similar magnitude. To the extent that developing coherence is difficult in your company, a crisis can at least force you to take a big leap forward.

Frugality for the Long Run

Having cut what isn't essential, how do you ensure that it stays cut? *Expense creep* is a sign that incoherence is returning to your company—or perhaps that it never went away. Your best response, even in good times and even when there's less pressure, is to continue evaluating your costs in light of your way to play.

That's what JCI did. For many years after its Sears-induced crisis, its executives were still holding monthly get-togethers to talk about what might be changing in their business. Those sessions allowed them to conduct ongoing cost assessments and make the needed adjustments—without unexpected layoffs or draconian measures, but also without returning to their old losses.

One valuable lesson from both the JCI and RJR examples—indeed, from every case we know—is a statement we made at the beginning of this chapter. Costs and strategy are inseparable. Every investment, whether good or bad, counts. On one hand, only by assessing costs regularly and consistently can you develop an ingrained awareness of your capabilities system and its relationship to other expenses. On the other, only by being clear about your way to play and capabilities system can you ensure a long-term, sustainable, good cost position. Without that clarity, you will always be tempted to overinvest in the wrong places.

In the final part of the book, we'll look more closely at the processes needed to develop a capabilities-driven strategy. Chapter 10, in particular, walks through the steps from start to finish. We hope we've shown that linking costs with coherence is not only a smart thing to do. It's the only way you'll realize your aspirations.

IV

LIVING COHERENCE
EVERY DAY

CHAPTER TEN

THE ESSENTIAL ADVANTAGE ROAD MAP

In this chapter, we lay out the road map for a capabilities-driven strategy initiative: the journey to essential advantage. Having come this far, we assume that you recognize the value of this approach, and that you already have an idea of your relative coherence, compared with competitors. Perhaps you have already taken the Coherence Test (table 3-1). In any case, you are ready to develop a more effective way to play and a capabilities system and draw them together with your critical products and services.

A handpicked team of core people should by now be dedicated to the strategy process, overseen by a team composed of most or all of the senior executives of your company. During the next several months, these two groups will work through the five stages of activity that we described briefly in chapter 3. These are: discovery (developing a comprehensive understanding of your situation and formulating hypotheses for your way to play); assessment (testing and refining those hypotheses); choice (making a full commitment to an overall strategic direction); transformation (setting in motion the actions needed to bring that strategy to life); and evolution (continually developing your new strategy and further creating and capturing value).

This design reflects a shift we see in business today—from treating strategy as an answer, handed down from a group of experts (inside or outside), to strategy as an ongoing process, with the management team and business leaders engaged and driving the organization forward.

Before Beginning the Journey

As your first important decision, consider your scale and scope of activity: where to begin and what markets to address. Specifically, will you conduct this work at the full-enterprise level or within just a part of your company? (That part could be a business unit or a group that faces a single market.)

Starting at a more local level won't move your entire organization to full coherence, but it is often an easy and pragmatic entry point for strategic change. You can test the waters here before committing the enterprise to an overarching strategic shift. A business unit can then become a pocket of coherence: a springboard for broader change. Be sure to explicitly identify the part of the organization that will participate, and the markets you hope to address, so there is no confusion about who is involved.

If the senior management and board are interested in major performance improvement or a leap to new forms of growth, then you might begin with a full-enterprise exercise, working across multiple business units and divisions to develop a common capabilities-driven strategy. This process is typically as all-encompassing and intensive as a major reorganization or merger. In one such initiative for the North American unit of a company with more than a half-dozen lines of business and annual revenue in excess of $10 billion, there were eighteen planned workshops and input sessions in a span of four months, including two board discussions. Though it may start at the corporate center, an enterprise-wide capabilities-driven strategy initiative will expand to involve discussions in every part of your company. (For more detail about enterprise-level strategies, see the end of this chapter.)

Whatever its scale, a capabilities-driven strategy requires the full approval and involvement of those to whom you're accountable. At the enterprise level, this means the board. Before you begin, gauge the board's appetite for near-term profit trade-offs—giving up seemingly profitable businesses or making investments now for the sake of coherence and its benefits later—and for capital-structure changes if your agenda calls for acquisitions. At a business-unit or other local level, you'll need the CEO's and senior executive team's wholehearted endorsement, especially as you make some of those same trade-offs.

You'll also need engagement from below. People at every level will not just execute your strategy, but also conceive and develop new approaches and applications. If they misunderstand the intent of your way to play, they will not make decisions effectively. As the number of people involved in this strategy grows, you will reach coherence only by gaining the support of the natural leaders among them.

The entire process could take weeks, or months—perhaps six months or more. You need time to iterate, test, and confirm your views, and most of all to gain the confidence to make a full commitment to your new strategy. If you expect your strategic choices to have significant impact, then this time will not be wasted. The "Checklist for Starting the Journey" poses further questions that will help you embark on this initiative.

CHECKLIST FOR STARTING THE JOURNEY

1. What is your agenda—your objective in terms of value creation? Start by articulating a clear, simple idea of what you hope to achieve—for example, doubling or tripling enterprise value. How will coherence help you reach this goal? What else do you hope to change? Is there a "burning platform" (a crisis of some sort) that must be addressed? How will you define your relevant market (taking into account the "substitutes" described in chapter 3)?

As we have seen, you don't need to achieve complete coherence to create value. Keep your aspirations high, but also remind people that any movement toward relative coherence will lead to tangible gains along the way.

2. Who will lead the initiative? For the core team, appoint experienced executives. Include functional leaders essential to the discussion and senior line executives from relevant business units. The composition of the team may change as you progress, but some core team members should remain constant, owning the initiative and taking responsibility for the outcome. Involve representatives from most or all parts of the company, along with other relevant groups such as key suppliers and customers, so that the team's work is relevant to (and credible with) a broad group of constituents. Above all, choose people who recognize the value of coherence and their own potential role in building it. Make sure their other responsibilities are at least partly covered, so that this important role is not seen as an inappropriately demanding extra burden.

3. How will the top leaders be involved? If you are the chief executive or division head to whom the core team reports, make it clear from the start that this will be a hands-on activity for you and the other leading executives on your senior team. A capabilities-driven strategy is an exercise in boldly and decisively reframing the basic choices for your company in a way that you, and the rest of the company, must stand behind for years. No one can speak for the whole as effectively as you and your peers can.

The Discovery Stage

Like the discovery phase of a legal case, this stage involves setting a context for action. It takes place through a series of intensive, highly engaging discussions and workshops: optimally conducted over several weeks with the same core team of ten to twenty people. In these sessions, you explore and develop a shared understanding of three basic realities that affect your way to play: your customers and competitors (a market-back view), your potential growth opportunities (an aspirational view of market attractiveness), and your own distinctive strengths relative to your competitors (a capabilities-forward perspective). From all of the complexities inherent in these realities, you synthesize a group of clear, cogent hypotheses: each one a potential way to play that could be viable for you.

Stage 1: Discover

Deliverable: Three to five initial hypotheses for distinct way-to-play options.

Roles

Senior management: Define objectives, set criteria, direction, and boundaries (some ways to play may not be appropriate for reasons that senior management establishes).

Core team: Explore and analyze your markets, potential growth paths, and capabilities; synthesize way-to-play hypotheses; recommend ways to play to assess in the next stage. Tools and exercises: Winners and losers (see below), puretones (chapter 4, table 4-1), market dynamics (table 10-1), growth types (chapter 7, figure 7-1), coherence test (chapter 3, table 3-1), capabilities inventory, decision history (see below).

Broader organization: Contribute data and perspectives.

Key Questions

Way to play: How are you and your competitors playing in the market right now? Who is winning? Who is losing? What are your major growth opportunities? What alternative ways to play might be worth considering?

Capabilities system: Can you articulate the three to six capabilities at which you excel? How could they support a potential way to play?

Products and services: How aligned are your products and services with your current way to play and capabilities system?

Essential advantage: How is your company performing relative to other players? How do different members of the senior team answer these questions? Are your perceptions aligned with one another's and with the market?

The first three substeps of the discovery stage—focused respectively on market, growth, and capabilities—can be conducted either in sequence or in parallel. They must be separate enough that the team benefits from disparate perspectives, and intertwined enough that ideas can be carried from one to the other. This is not a cumbersome, "boil the ocean"–style deductive process in which you gather and analyze mountains of new data. Rather, it's an inductive approach in which you draw on the insights you already have to brainstorm and explore potential ways to play. In the fourth substep of this stage, when you bring together the insights you have gained, you will have a chance to settle on the three to five hypotheses that you will assess more closely in the next stage.

In all the discovery-stage sessions that you conduct, make it a goal to develop greater clarity about your own business. An open tone and candid informality is as important as the content. Don't dismiss any hypothesis too rapidly; perhaps it contradicts your ingrained way of thinking, but reveals challenges or opportunities that you shouldn't overlook. Make room for blue-sky thinking; if it helps, draw on examples of remarkable innovative leaps, such as P&G's Swiffer mop or Tata's $2,400 Nano automobile. Cultivate an expanded definition of your business (you don't sell copiers; you're in information management). Then come back to earth to think more pragmatically about your business realities today.

Market-Back Discovery

As in any "market-back" study, focus on customers, potential customers, regulators, and competitors. In several different exercises, you gain a more focused understanding of your business context and how the world is changing. In the process, hypotheses for potential ways to play will emerge.

Winners and losers: Use the coherence test template (table 3-1) to look closely at your competitors' market position compared to your own. Who is the market rewarding—in other words, who has a right to win? What ways to play have they adopted? (Combine the puretone examples in table 4-1 to describe these.) What are their growth rates? What capabilities systems enable their success? This discussion brings to life your current level of coherence compared to that of your competitors. You may discover that even the most successful businesses in a sector are not fully coherent.

Market dynamics: Use some or all of the indicators in table 10-1 to develop hypotheses for new ways to play. Your goal is specific: to recognize potential ways to play that will be available in your market in the future. Look at trends and drivers, seeking a deeper understanding of how your market has behaved up until now, how it is changing, and if the current winners will keep winning. The various tests in this table explore the ways in which your customer base is growing or shrinking; your materials are getting more scarce (or more plentiful); your competitors are thriving or struggling; and so on. Pick the tests that seem likely to offer fresh insights about potential ways to play. In applying these tests, beware of jumping to conclusions that may limit the range of options you consider. In particular, avoid the temptation of trying to size the market for your products and services. At this early stage, sizing the market can bias you toward large populations and make it hard to see the value of other markets, which could turn out to be more viable and profitable for you.

Puretones: Look at the puretone ways to play, as listed in table 4-1. Walk down the list, considering each in turn, asking which resonate with the insights from your winners and losers and market dynamics discussions, or with your general sense of viable growth options. Then talk through the implications of each puretone. For example, if you wanted to be an experience provider, which customers would you try to reach? What would be the most compelling

TABLE 10-1

Market dynamics to consider when assessing your way to play

Costs

Market dynamic	Measures and indicators	Implications for your way to play
Competitive cost positions and variability	Variability among suppliers in the cost of producing a given product or service; competitive cost positions derived from supply curves, experience curves, and relative scale	If the cost variation is narrowing, this sector may be moving toward a painful commoditization around prices. If the variations are great or growing, there may be more differentiated ways to play or an opportunity for a stronger value player to emerge. Cost structure variability can also reflect an immature market. As producers become more efficient, they will force out marginal players, reducing prices for all.
Relative scarcity of materials	Price volatility for and availability of critical materials	If, for example, the price of lithium goes up, electric-vehicle manufacturers would fare better as innovators or premium players. If the price of diamonds goes up, there is also opportunity for integrators and risk avoiders who can help their customers manage supply. Volatile raw-material prices indicate the need for a capability to hedge risk through financial instruments. A spot-pricing capability is also useful to maximize profit by adjusting product price and availability in times of shortages. For example, video game consoles have successfully sold for hundreds of dollars more per unit during times of microprocessor scarcity.

Customers

Market dynamic	Measures and indicators	Implications for your way to play
Price tiers	Number of price points in a sector or industry	If the range of prices grows smaller, the market may be commoditizing or consolidating, or there may be substitution, as consumers move to another product or service. If the range grows larger, there may be untapped opportunities for premium or experience providers as the segment grows. In a sector like personal electronics, the number of price tiers for a category may indicate the full range of consumer interests—and thus an opportunity for customizers (which can match an individual's wishes) and aggregators (which

Customers

Market dynamic	Measures and indicators	Implications for your way to play
		can simplify the selection process). Also look for changes in overall prices, either up or down: for newspapers and magazines, the launch of Craigslist and discount Web advertising led to a price-tier change in ad revenues and, in effect, signaled that the industry's way to play would have to change.
Price variance	Range of prices paid for ostensibly similar products or services	High price variance may be due to differences in channel economics; the same product will sell for different prices in 7-Eleven and Walmart. This can also indicate an immature market, with suppliers getting higher prices for scarce products (in time, competition will bring those prices in line) or the value accrued to a reputation or premium player, such as Nordstrom. High variance may also indicate that solutions providers or experience providers are active in this market.
Purchase volume volatility	Sales volume changes over time, adjusted for pricing changes	Snack foods and fashion apparel are examples of sectors with high purchase-volume volatility; consumers continually want new flavors, new packaging, or new experiences. Changes in purchase volume may be driven by consumers' dissatisfaction with the options from current providers, suggesting an opportunity to create loyalty or simply fulfill demand through innovation. Or there may be a substitute problem, with competition coming from outside the narrowly defined category. Low volatility indicates a maturing market, with levels of customer satisfaction that could present barriers to entry for newcomers, unless they can deliver significant new value.
Market share volatility	Changes in market share among players	High levels of market share volatility can indicate lack of customer loyalty or commoditization (that's why customers may be switching brands frequently); an entrant or existing player may need to bring in a new quality or feature to attract loyal users.
Product turnover rates	In a particular sector, the average time between the release of new products, and the average time	Landline (slow) and cellular (fast) phones present a fascinating contrast in product turnover rates and the implied way to play for companies in that sector. The slower the product

(continued)

TABLE 10-1 (*continued*)

Customers

Market dynamic	Measures and indicators	Implications for your way to play
	before consumers replace or repurchase products	turnover rate, the more an innovator must rely on major game-changers that shift the way consumers use a product or service—for example, the P&G Swiffer mop or the replacement of coal power plants with natural gas. Slow product turnover can also indicate consumer satisfaction, consolidating supply or monopoly power—for example, Microsoft releases new versions of Windows at a relatively slow pace.

Competitors

Market dynamic	Measures and indicators	Implications for your way to play
Value chain complexity	Number of available distribution and supply channels	If the value chain is small, this may present opportunities for a disinter-mediator; if it is large, it may present opportunities for an aggregator or integrator.
Regulatory impact	Value influenced by regulation or govern-ment oversight	If this is high, regulatory management may be required in your capabilities system if you compete in this market (or it may just be table stakes, depending on your way to play). Incumbents will try to limit the pace of market liberalization by regulators, while new entrants lobby for increased liberalization to gain advantage against incumbents.
Entrant rate for new players	Number of companies entering this sector over time	High frequency of entrants may suggest an opportunity for distinctive ways to play (as in the aerospace and defense industry after the Cold War) or dissatis-faction with the current prevailing ways to play. It may also simply represent a prevailing belief that this sector is profitable—with a growing market, attractive margins, or rapidly evolving customer preferences.

market? How would it be different from your current (implicit or explicit) way to play? As part of this exercise, you may also hit on a puretone that isn't on the list or hasn't been conceived yet. That's fine; write down your description of it, for consideration among the other possible options.

Opportunities for Growth

As a way to engage people and form more hypotheses, brainstorm a list of opportunities for growth. Include ideas you have considered in the past and new approaches; seek out ideas from people around the company. Look again at the market dynamics analyses in table 10-1: Do any of them suggest possible growth avenues?

For a more structured way to brainstorm about growth, look at the four growth types outlined in chapter 7 (see figure 7-1). Work your way outward from the center. Are there places where you can find added headroom for growth, with your existing lineup of products and services? Are there adjacencies to pursue—products or services close to yours, that would make use of your existing capabilities or capabilities system? Where are the most promising candidates for geographic expansion? What new platforms for growth could be built by transforming your business entirely? Cast your list of growth paths broadly at first. Then narrow it to those that seem most promising.

Capabilities-Forward Discovery

In this sub-step, look at possible ways to play from a "capabilities-forward" angle. Focus on the things your company does well, and derive hypotheses accordingly. This is a critical part of the process, because, for the first time, you are considering potential ways to play and capabilities in light of one another.

Conduct a capabilities inventory: What is your company known for doing exceptionally well? Conversely, what have your competitors been able to do that you can't match? How are your capabilities changing? Are they improving or declining?

Scan the puretones (table 4-1) for ways to play that would logically make use of your most distinctive capabilities: You can also use a timeline-based discussion to look at your capabilities in more depth, and to get a sense of which ways to play could fit with your culture and identity (see the "Decision History" box).

DECISION HISTORY

Any variation of this exercise can be useful in your capabilities-forward discovery process. On a timeline posted on a conference room wall, trace the history of the last twenty to forty major decisions made by the management of your company and the rationales behind them. Alternatively, look at the history of the last year's worth of leadership team meetings (using the agendas to refresh your memory), or the last ten years' worth of major project launches and new initiatives.

As each participant describes events, record them in the appropriate spots on the timeline. For each one, ask: Was it coherent with the stated strategy of the time? How did it come about? What were the effects? Some of these moves undoubtedly involved the introduction of new technologies, processes, products, and services. Others may have involved the launch or development of critical capabilities. Which turned out to be useful investments and why?

You may discover some components of your current strategy that no longer serve a purpose. "Oh, that product was developed by a regional marketing team, and they're no longer here." Or, regarding a supply chain capability that few companies use: "You mean we haven't shut that down yet?" There is usually plenty of laughter as the chronology gets filled in, but also an appreciation of the measures that worked along the way and an enhanced awareness of the coherence (and incoherence) that you have in common.[a]

[a]Adapted from Rick Ross and Art Kleiner, "The History Map," in *The Dance of Change,* by Peter Senge et al. (New York: Doubleday, 1999), 186.

Synthesis of Hypotheses

Inevitably, as you go through the discovery stage, hypotheses for ways to play will emerge. You will find yourselves testing them informally, thinking about which ones are feasible and what investments they would require. Now, in the final workshop, you bring all these insights together: combining your list of possibilities from the market dynamics exercise, your list of puretones, and your list of growth hypotheses, along with any others. Talk through them all, and settle on three to five way-to-play hypotheses to take to the next stage.

The process of synthesis is neither purely analytical nor intuitive. As William Duggan of Columbia Business School has observed, most creative synthesis involves drawing new links, in your mind, from what you observe now to what you know from experience. Trust that this type of insight will kick in as you discuss the hypotheses you have developed.[1]

Combine puretones into new hypotheses. Draw on what you've learned about your company and your market. Look for ways to play that resonate on all three dimensions: market-facing, geared toward growth, and relevant to your capabilities. But don't limit yourself too much; follow your collective sense of the most effective hypotheses, rather than any checklist. For example, feel free to keep an extremely valuable way to play in the mix even if it's not clear how it would fit with your capabilities. You will seek coherence more explicitly in the next stage.

The final ways to play that you select should differ enough from one another that a casual observer could easily distinguish them. For example, if you have two hypotheses for being a value player, combine them into one. Don't worry too much about the details; they will be refined iteratively in the next stage. The hypotheses should also be compelling enough that you can make a powerful story out of each of them, and be applicable to your own business and market.

Give each of the working hypotheses a name and write up a description of them all—and how they fit with the market factors, growth opportunities, and capabilities you've considered. Then take it to the senior team for approval. In the next two stages—assessment and choice—the core team and senior team, along with others throughout the company, will invest a great deal of time and effort in clarifying, iterating, and refining this list so that it becomes easier to make a choice.

The Assessment Stage

This is the stage of due diligence: you dig deeper into the issues that were raised in the discovery stage and validate your hypotheses. Test them with an eye toward the amount of enterprise value they might create and their feasibility. To accomplish this, evaluate each hypothesis through four lenses: its fit with your capabilities system; the way it positions you against competitors (your right to win); its financial prospects; and the risks you would be undertaking by pursuing it. As the research and discussion continue, revise the descriptions of these hypotheses to reflect what you are learning, and discard those that are not feasible. These assessments, conducted by the core team, represent vital input for the choices that must be made in stage 3.

Stage 2: Assess

Deliverable: Assessment of how much value would be created by adopting each way to play and the risks entailed in capturing that value.

Roles

Senior management: Guide and validate assessments throughout this stage.

Core team: Conduct interviews and analyses; further develop way-to-play hypotheses for senior management consideration. Tools and exercises: Interviews; assessing your capabilities (see below); right-to-win exercise (table 10-2); assessing your financial prospects (see below); assessing potential risk (see below).

Broader organization: Support analysis upon request.

Key Questions

Way to play: How attractive (and relevant to you) are the alternative ways to play?

Capabilities system: For each way to play, could you build advantage with your capabilities? Would these capabilities give you a right to win? If not, what capabilities would you have to obtain or develop? How would you feasibly do it?

Products and services: For each way to play, how would it help your products and services to thrive?

Essential advantage: How does each way to play differentiate your company?

The five sub-steps of this stage are all conducted by the core team. This time, they must occur in sequence, with the insights from each informing the others. As you work through these forms of assessment, we recommend also conducting at least a dozen interviews: ideally, two for each functional area of the business and some with select trusted customers or supply partners. During these interviews, discuss the strategies you are considering, their potential in value creation, and the capabilities and assets needed to make them work. Ask whether, in light of their observations and experience, your company is equipped to deliver this way to play, and why.

Though a formal review by the executive team isn't necessary (that will take place in stage 3), it's important to have clear, regular lines of communication so that the CEO and other leading executives can monitor the way the hypotheses are developing and offer guidance. Indeed, some members of the executive team may want to join the core team for some of these sessions.

Assessing Your Capabilities System

For each leading hypothesis, articulate the capabilities system it would require, the relevant capabilities that you already have available to your company—including those you have in-house, can draw on through alliances or outsourcing, or could reasonably develop to a distinctive level—and the relevant capabilities that you don't have, that you would have to build organically or acquire (or both) to make this way to play work.

For example, a solutions provider might need to be great at (1) product assembly close to customers, (2) forecasting component demand, (3) online retailing, and (4) responsive and flexible supply-chain management. An experience provider might bring to bear (1) an understanding of how people interact with the product, (2) consumer-centered technology and design innovation, (3) distinctive branding, and (4) expert management of the customer experience. And the mutually reinforcing capabilities for a value player might be (1) demand forecasting, (2) component selection and procurement, (3) lean and efficient supply-chain management, (4) management of relationships with retailers, and (5) expertise in understanding the features valued by customers.

Separate the distinctive capabilities that would be needed to make each way to play work from the table stakes. For the most critical capabilities, estimate the amount of investment that would be required to give your company the distinction it needs in that domain. If too many gaps need closing, then ask whether you can really change enough to deliver the capabilities to win with this way to play—and if the answer is no, discard that hypothesis. Conversely, the more advantaged your capabilities system compared with those of competitors, the more promising the option.

Assessing Your Right to Win

As you may recall from earlier chapters, the right to win is the confidence held by companies with more coherence than their competitors. In this substep, you look at every way-to-play hypothesis in light of your own relative coherence against that of your competitors. Which company brings the right combination of a capabilities system that the market wants and the assets that are needed to succeed?

The "right-to-win exercise" shown in table 10-2 can help you clarify this assessment. For each way-to-play hypothesis, create a separate table based on this worksheet. Assess your capabilities and assets alongside those of your main competitors (and for new markets, consider potential entrants).

Although assets are not as sustainable as capabilities, we include them in this worksheet because they represent criteria that are important to the market. The worksheet also separates your distinctive capabilities (those which, as part of your capabilities system, enable your way to play) from table stakes. For instance, if you are a manufacturer, you may need some assets, such as facilities and patents. You will also need a table-stakes proficiency at distribution and logistics. These may

TABLE 10-2

The right-to-win exercise

In this exercise, you assess your own company and those of your competitors on various capabilities, assets, and other activities. Rate them as above par, at par, or below par. (See explanation in the text of chapter 10.)

Differentiating capabilities system (list up to 6)	Your company	Competitor 1	Competitor 2
Capability 1	...	...	...
Capability 2			
Capability 3			
Capability 4			
Capability 5			
Capability 6			
Rating			

Differentiating assets	Your company	Competitor 1	Competitor 2
Asset 1			
Asset 2			
Rating			

Table-stakes activities	Your company	Competitor 1	Competitor 2
Activity 1			
Activity 2			
Activity 3			
Rating			
Total rating			

not, however, represent the distinctive capabilities that set you apart from rivals. You don't need to be above par on a table-stakes activity; you just want to be as proficient as the market demands. (Indeed, being above par on a table-stakes activity suggests you are overinvesting, which we have addressed in chapter 9.)

Rate yourself and your competitors (current or potential) for each element on your list: above par, at par, or below par. To keep track of the many elements in this discussion, use colors: green for above par, yellow for par, and red for below par. In developing these assessments, you will probably draw on interviews, analysis, and your own open, dispassionate discussions about your right to win, how plausible your assessment of it is, and how many gaps need to be addressed.

For an interactive version of these exercises, visit
www.theessentialadvantage.com.

One analogue for this exercise is the analysis that Wharton School marketing professor George S. Day suggests for evaluating potential investment in new products. (He, too, advises teams to ask not just "Is the market real?" and "Is it worth doing?" but also "Can we win?") It's not easy to bring the necessary perspective to bear, to be dispassionate and honest. "A critical job," says Day, "is preventing teams from regarding the [exercise] as an obstacle to be overcome or circumvented . . . It is a learning tool for revealing dubious assumptions and identifying problems and solutions."[2]

Assessing Your Financial Prospects

In the discovery stage, you associated potential growth options with each way-to-play hypothesis. Now assess those growth options, as a group, to conduct a realistic estimate of the potential economic value. (In some companies, there might be sixty or more growth options on the table, each linked to one or more hypotheses.) How might these growth options affect revenues and profits? What would be the financial upside? How large might the potential market be, when sized in terms of revenue, profit, and impact on enterprise value? Where are the economies of scale? Use all of the traditional analyses that are credible in your business: market size, return on investment, enterprise value, and so on. Make sure to provide the rationale for your estimates so that others understand your thinking. Then, tally up your estimates to get a comparable view, for each way-to-play hypothesis, of its financial potential as a whole.

Assessing Potential Risk

Make a clear-eyed assessment of everything that could go wrong for each way-to-play hypothesis. What are the risks of reputational damage, legal liability, or financial loss? Could the risks hurt the profitability of your biggest and most successful current businesses? If the change you're contemplating would require a major restructuring, do you clearly understand what this would entail, and do you have confidence in your ability to carry it off? Would your existing customers be hurt?

Every company, of course, needs to take risks to grow. The value of this exercise comes from establishing a clearer view of the trade-off between risk and reward for each way-to-play hypothesis. Ultimately, it will be up to the most senior executives to decide which overall rewards would be worth the risk. For that reason, once the risks have been initially identified, it is valuable to conduct a joint session with the core and executive teams, to determine which risks need further research and analysis before making a decision.

Deliberation and Presentation

By the end of stage 2, the members of your core team should be able to speak to the merits and risks of each way to play and its associated capabilities system. You should be confident that any of the hypotheses you present could become viable ways to play, worthy of strong consideration. There should be a logical rationale for each, showing that, if designed and executed well, it could lead to a right to win.

The Choice Stage

You've been at work for two months or more—perhaps several months. Your hypotheses have turned into full-scale options. You have in mind several ways to play. You are aware of the capabilities system that might be necessary for each way to play. You have thought about the products and services that would fit with these. Now it's time for your top executives to review the assessments made in stage 2 and pick a strategy that is more coherent. In short, you now make a commitment to the sustainable future the company will create.

The choice of a way to play and capabilities system is not like most of the other business decisions that you make. It is a fundamental commitment to your objectives and targets, and the logic underlying them. This choice will become the basis of many priorities. It will determine the way you resolve many day-to-day conflicts. It will generate the essential advantage that your organization needs. It should not be treated as an ordinary decision.

Stage 3: Choose

Deliverable: A fully agreed-upon capabilities-driven strategy.

Roles

Senior management: Choose and commit to a way to play, capabilities system, and related objectives and targets.

Core team: Recommend a way to play. Tools and exercises: Strategic debate workshop, alternative futures, stress tests, or other review exercises (see below).

Broader organization: Support the development of business cases.

Key Questions

Way to play: Which way to play do you choose?

Capabilities system: Will your capabilities system support your right to win?

Products and services: What is the agreed-upon product and service portfolio? What is the general timeline for making these changes?

Essential advantage: What are your criteria for judging the success of your new efforts?

As a result of this choice, some brands and services will almost certainly rise in importance, and people working in these businesses will gain a huge morale boost. Other product and service groups will face tougher times. Henceforth, they won't have the same level of investment funneled toward them; some may be divested or shut down. Some major functional initiatives you had slated for next year may no longer be differentiating; they will be halted.

It is thus natural to feel a little exposed when making this choice. But if you have managed stages 1 and 2 effectively, you should have confidence in your decision. You are taking a fundamental leap of faith, but it is supported by your experience and the work you and your team have done.

Typically, this stage begins with the core team recommending an option. To get to that point, three exercises are relevant. In some companies, these sessions have been so valuable that they go on for two or more days—giving people a chance to sleep on the implications. Any of the three might serve your purpose:

- *Strategic debate workshop:* The case for adopting each way to play is advocated by a different member of the team, often drawing on the knowledge gained from his or her existing position. The head of finance might argue for becoming a consolidator, the head of marketing might advocate the reputation-player route, and the head of operations might speak for the fast-follower option. Each leader paints a picture of what that way to play would accomplish; the capabilities system that would be required for success; how it would offer differential value to customers; and how to fill the gaps in capabilities, assets, products, and services.

- *Alternative futures:* Different members of the core team present narratives for each prospective way to play, looking backward from five years in the future. What happened, as a result of taking this path? What challenges did your company face? What capabilities did you have to acquire or develop? Where did you see your greatest competition? With as much substantiation as possible, how successful did this path turn out to be, and why? Imagine a newspaper headline about your company, based on your pursuit of this way to play. Does it depict you as dominant in your industry, as a takeover target, or as somewhere in between?

- *Stress tests:* Look at the challenges and potential rewards for each alternative way to play. What challenges do you face around capital markets; environmental, safety, or health considerations; personnel and talent issues; global and local competition; and disruptive technologies? What is the plausible range of market share and profitability available under each way to play? Compare them all to see how they stand up against similar challenges.

However you design these workshops, the chief executive and the senior team should be present for the final iteration—because ultimately the decision rests with them. In this session (and any follow-up sessions that are needed), the senior team should settle on the following components of your company's strategy:

- A chosen way to play and capabilities system, and a first take on the products and services that fit this "sweet spot." (If it's a large enterprise, you may choose to divide your company into separate clusters, each with its own way to play and capabilities system—but do so consciously, knowing that you will have to compensate for the incoherence that this split creates.)

- Preliminary options and directions for the ways in which you will create value—through growth, M&A, and reducing unnecessary costs—so that you can invest more heavily in the capabilities that matter.

- Criteria for judging your success. Some criteria may simply represent higher performance—an increase of ten points in market share, a doubling of revenue growth, or a specified level of cash flow. Others may reflect your chosen capabilities—the attraction of certain types of customers (for an experience player), turnover time for product launches (for an innovator), or margins compared with competitors (for a value player). These criteria are not meant to force results, but are meant to help build judgment about your progress.

- A general migration path to your chosen way to play. As part of this, the senior team needs to make an explicit commitment, both to the result and to the remaining time and effort that it will take to realize this strategy.

You have presumably gone through this exercise aware of the benefits of reaching one single way to play and capabilities system, with the coherence premium that provides. Nonetheless, at the broader enterprise level, there may be reasons one way to play is not pragmatic right now. Even if you choose just one, there may be a long migration path ahead of you. Remember, in either case, that in creating value, relative coherence is what matters. If you are planning to retain more than one way to play, talk openly about the tradeoffs. How will this affect your ability to invest in the capabilities that matter? How will it distract you? How can you gain the clarity you need against more focused competitors?

During the choice stage and in all subsequent stages, especially if you are the CEO or a senior leader, keep in mind that everything you say, do, and pay attention to will be closely watched—even more closely than usual. Others will expect you to hold to these commitments. If you are not visibly paying attention to the strategy you have chosen, no one else will, and for good reason: they would be making themselves vulnerable by embracing major changes that the top executives do not fully support. Conversely, if you do make a full commitment, then you establish a model for new behaviors throughout your company—the kind of behaviors you will need if the strategy is to work.

The Transformation Stage

A senior executive during this stage, surveying a wall-sized list of things that had to be done, turned to the rest of the team and said, "What do we do first? We can't do it all right now." One deliverable in this stage is a plan that answers that question: how you expect to build the capabilities you need, change your investment plans, design new organizational structures and practices, and adjust your portfolio—and in what order? The other deliverable is your initial actions: several highly visible moments of truth, which set in motion the necessary transformation that will allow you to realize your way to play. By the end of the transformation stage, your company will probably have shifted its hierarchy, recast goals and incentives, reallocated resources to the key capabilities, launched detailed plans to capture the primary growth avenues that were identified, and reprioritized R&D projects. These decisions will demonstrate to everyone that you are moving toward coherence.

Stage 4: Transform

Deliverable: Plan for change and first action steps.

Roles

Senior management: Decide on your portfolio changes, growth and capability-building initiatives, and growth and cost moves; adjust your operating model and organizational structure; and begin seeding the necessary conversations.

Core team: Develop a plan for the portfolio changes and their execution. Develop a communications strategy for top executives to help them make sure everybody gets the message. Tools and exercises: Portfolio matrix (figure 6-1); estimating your headroom for growth (chapter 7); process for cutting costs (chapter 9).

Broader organization: Participate in and support the plan development. Throughout the organization, this is the time for subgroups, teams, and project leaders to align their action plans with your overall strategy and set up appropriate initiatives. Tools and exercises: Right-to-win matrix (earlier in this chapter); portfolio matrix (figure 6-1).

Key Questions

Way to play: How does each part of the business apply this way to play? How do you mobilize and focus the organization?

Capabilities system: How do you build, develop, or buy the capabilities you need but don't have? How can your operating model support your capabilities system?

Products and services: What parts of the business should you expand? What parts should you divest? How will you prepare your organization for portfolio changes?

Essential advantage: What are you going to do differently to live coherence every day? How will you budget new performance expectations and monitor results? What trends or external forces might affect your way to play and capabilities system?

You're crossing a threshold into a new order that must be planned for and developed deliberately. Everything is still new. Perhaps that's why this tends to be one of the most enjoyable parts of the process for the executives involved: a great moment when you roll out the choice, reorganize the company around it, and see a wide range of activity begin, all moving toward greater harmony.

At the same time, no matter how prepared you are, the transition is challenging. Others in the company are waiting to see if you blink. They want to know if they can follow your lead full-heartedly, without fear of wasting their efforts. They also want to know, as you reorganize, what will happen to their positions, projects, and prospects.

The development of plans might last several months and involve discussions at many levels. At the executive level, there will be many pressing questions to answer. How do you expect to preserve the value of parts of the company that won't stay in the portfolio, and how can you get a good price for them? As you move your investments toward the capabilities that really matter, where will spending reductions be expected? What kind of knowledge must be codified to improve the capabilities in your system, and how will that be managed?

The core team, and others, may also get involved in organizational change plans. The process could include identifying and reaching out for the key champions, developing large-scale ways to help people model new behaviors, and assessing leadership capacity. Leaders in each region or business unit may need to talk through their ideas about value creation, growth, M&A, and cost-cutting. Given the choice of an overarching way to play and capabilities system, what changes should take place in these arenas? What new formal structures, informal networks, channels of communication, cultural change efforts, and forms of recruiting and talent management are needed? Some members of the core team may move into a facilitative role at this stage, working with people throughout the company to help them develop capabilities-driven strategies for their parts of the business.

The "moments of truth" will be decisions and actions that signal to everyone the magnitude and direction of the change. Several good examples are available from Jack Welch's tenure as CEO of GE. Soon after he took office in 1981, he eliminated 80 percent of the strategic planning staff positions. During the next three years, he divested 117 business units, culminating in the sale of GE Housewares, its small appliance business, to Black & Decker in 1984. As Noel Tichy and Stratford Sherman put it, this was a failing business with little connection to GE's capabilities or overall strategy, but it was an iconic enterprise for people in the company, because they could see their logo on alarm clocks and hair curlers in homes around the world. The sale of GE Housewares sparked a "process of self-discovery at GE, forcing unexamined issues into the open. For the first time in memory, employees throughout the company seriously began to ponder GE's mission, questioning assumptions and discussing the unspoken."[3]

Something similar may happen in your company as you create your own moments of truth: your first bold moves toward coherence. Expect to conduct lots of conversations and to encounter both overt and covert skepticism and resistance. One afternoon, you face your boss (or a board member) questioning why a profitable brand must be sold. The next morning, you kill several innovative projects over the cries of their champions. "Sorry, it doesn't fit," you have to say. Or, "We have more potential in this other way to play, which means we're getting rid of some of the capabilities you were counting on."

You can also count on sparking people's enthusiasm and interest. Now that you've put your stake in the ground and it is clear to everyone where the company (or the division) is going, you will find many people climbing on board. They understand that they have a better future in a company that is coherent, and it is up to you now to execute that future with the same care and consideration that you put into determining it. The more you can get your valuable people engaged (including those whose projects were killed), the more effective the overall transformation stage will be.

The Evolution Stage

By the evolution stage, your company has entered its "new normal": it is pursuing its new way to play, exercising its capabilities system, and experiencing the right to win firsthand. In this stage, you become a company that "lives coherence every day," following through with the practices and relationships that enable the capabilities system that delivers your way to play. At the same time, the world is changing—sometimes discontinuously—around you. A variety of challenges will come up that cause you to apply your strategy in new ways. Thus you continue to make decisions that reinforce coherence and prevent you from slipping back into your earlier fragmented state.

Stage 5: Evolve

Deliverable: Ongoing activity and continued commitment in support of the new way to play and capabilities system.

Roles

Senior management: Stay on message; continue to communicate and reinforce the strategy; live the moments of truth that continue to emerge; prevent incoherence from returning.

Core team: As they move into new roles, they become informal "stewards of coherence," focusing on culture change and monitoring ongoing progress.

Broader organization: Implement strategy; apply capabilities lens in day-to-day decisions.

Key Questions

Way to play: How do you stay aligned with market dynamics under this way to play?

Capabilities system: How can you continue to develop and improve your distinctive capabilities?

Products and services: What are your best growth and expansion options?

Essential advantage: How do you make it easier and easier for people to live coherence every day?

Though the details of this stage will vary dramatically from one company to the next, one principle remains constant: make it a continuing priority to apply your capabilities system to the greatest number of products and services within your way to play.

The evolution stage is nonprogrammatic: it never ends. But in its own way, it is as dramatic and significant as any of the previous stages. It involves continually adapting, improving, and extending the innovations; movements toward growth; and other practices that allow you to apply the capabilities you need. From here on, you write your own rulebook, and it should be coauthored by everyone who is committed to being part of your company's success.

In preparing for this journey, you need to consider two more topics: the changes needed in your organization (chapter 11), and the challenges of leadership (chapter 12).

FOR THE LEADERS OF AN ENTERPRISE-WIDE STRATEGY EXERCISE

When conducting a capabilities-driven strategy exercise at the enterprise level, with multiple businesses involved, who takes the lead—the corporate center, or the individual business units? In our experience, both teams participate. The source of initial momentum may be a function of how many business units you have. If you have only two or three business units, it may make sense to start there, working through separate strategies for each, and then bringing them together at the assessment stage. If you have a large number of business units involved, then the corporate core will need to take the lead.

When you are ready to begin making the choice, be as swift and decisive as possible, so that the businesses can begin the important work of discovery in their individual markets. Essentially, you are providing your businesses with a group of initial hypotheses you want them to consider, and you are eliminating some ways to play that you do not want teams to spend time on.

You should involve the heads of each business and function in this discussion, as the decisions you make now will limit the degrees of freedom these heads have as they explore their own market-based exercises. If they do not see a fit between the central hypotheses and their business, then you need to find out why and think about either revising your way-to-play hypotheses or treating this particular business as an outlier. (It may not fit with where the enterprise is going.) Either way, this important step enables your enterprise to move to more coherence, rather than have the overall strategy simply reflect the direction of each business.

The complexity of the enterprise situation means that corporate executives—including the CEO—must play a larger role. They must set the agenda, outlining any constraints and articulating the aspirations and goals that have brought the enterprise to this exercise ("Our level of capital investment cannot increase"; "We are looking to triple our revenues from emerging markets within five years"; "Our profitability improvements cannot come at the expense of customer satisfaction").

When combined with the efforts of the individual businesses, an exercise in developing an enterprise-wide capabilities-driven strategy will take longer than its single-market counterpart and involve many more constituents. The CEO will participate in many of the meetings, working with a core team of fellow executives and (on an as-needed basis) a supporting cast of business unit presidents, functional heads, specialized experts, and board members. Investors may also be involved; gauging shareholders' appetite for near-term profit trade-offs is important, as is gauging their tolerance for capital-structure changes. In particular, do you have the license from the capital markets to make major acquisitions?

Your choice, in stage 3, will incorporate recommendations from the critical business teams. Inevitably, you will choose an overall way to play that, in favoring the whole, appears closer to the interests of some businesses than others. If that's the case, you need to deal candidly with other questions: if the value-maximizing strategy for a given business would mean pursuing a different way to play, with a different capabilities system, from the rest of the enterprise, does this mean it should remain part of the portfolio? There will, of course, be borderline cases: businesses that need different table-stakes capabilities to succeed, but that can still use the enterprise's distinctive capabilities system to some degree. This is a good opportunity to consider the portfolio analysis in chapter 6 and to make clear decisions about what role each business will play.

To manage the complexity, you must stay close to the business teams throughout the process, and we recommend a regular senior team discussion to see how the hypotheses are evolving and which ways to play are emerging as front-runners. Again, you've chosen to pick up the problem at the enterprise level to build coherence, so these discussions become critical.

Finally, you need to make sure there's a strong organizational structure in place to manage these processes. In the next chapter, we'll look more closely at some of the innovations that can make this more feasible.

CHAPTER ELEVEN

ORGANIZING FOR COHERENCE

Most businesspeople have been through endless reorganizations. Each reorganization has its rationale, but rarely does it have anything to do with strategy. Some are intended to orient the business geographically; others to centralize activity toward headquarters; many to take out costs; still others to provide more autonomy to local business units. But few reorganizations are driven by the company's strategy. In fact, like cost, the topic of organization is usually seen as quite distinct from strategy.

What if, instead, you restructured your organizational hierarchy to support your way to play and to make the most of your capabilities system? Moreover, what if you deliberately set up informal conversations at every level to reinforce that new structure and to bring people on board? And what if your talent and recruitment policies and practices were explicitly built around finding and developing people with the knowledge to make your capabilities—and the businesses they fostered—world-class? If you could figure out how to do all this, you would reinforce your capabilities-driven company in powerful ways. Your company would, in effect, be living coherence every day.

You may already have an image in mind of what a capabilities-driven company looks like organizationally. If the image resembles ours, it's easy to describe. The company's people, from the top leadership on down, understand how their jobs fit with the overall strategic priorities. They take pride in the contribution they make to the company's capabilities system. A clear idea of the way to play, and the reasons it will succeed, is embedded in most everyday decisions and actions. People are confident that as part of a company with the right to win, they will be rewarded—collectively and individually. This in turn generates a prevailing mind-set that is optimistic, focused, and realistic about both the risks and the rewards of the company's strategy.

To foster this kind of company, you have several issues to think about:

1. How do you design an operating model and organizational structure that reinforces coherence and helps you build your capabilities system?

2. What must be done in the "informal" organization—the conversations you set in motion outside hierarchical boundaries—to foster coherence?

3. How do you need to change the way you manage talent: recruiting and developing people?

Let's look at each of these issues in turn.

Designing Coherent Structures

One of the first things the Pfizer Consumer Healthcare (PCH) division did when it pursued its claim-based way to play and capabilities system in the early 2000s was to reorganize around its capabilities. As you may recall from chapter 1, the business embraced six mutually reinforcing capabilities: new over-the-counter product launch and commercialization, claims-based marketing, effective retail execution, the ability to influence regulatory management and government policy, focused portfolio management of selected brands, and pharmaceutical-like innovation.

Unlike many reorganizations, this one "took." One reason for this was the reorganization's close link to the capabilities system; another was its freewheeling, experimental nature. Pfizer's leaders set up three different types of organizational mechanisms for their different capabilities. The first was a new type of portfolio management group; the second was a formal adaptation of informal networks; and the third was a new executive position to fill a gap in capability development.

In the area of portfolio management, PCH established a few specialized global teams to oversee its heavy-hitter, blockbuster "golden brands" (as they called them), such as Listerine, Nicorette, and Zyrtec. These were not add-ons; they were fully accountable for the success of their products. The golden brand teams were given their own budgeting authority, decision rights, and worldwide responsibility for profit and losses.

The rest of the products were managed by regional teams, which oversaw their strategies and controlled their marketing and operations. The regions—which oversaw the strategies for all the other PCH brands—could not opt out of what the golden brand teams decided. There was also deliberate crossover: each golden brand team included one representative from each regional organization and a chair who came from one of the regions.

The result was a structure that fed cooperation. The regional organizations remained accountable for the performance of the division as a whole, but they provided support to help supercharge the global brand teams. They had incentive to do this; bonuses were based in part on the contribution each person made to the capabilities-driven strategy.

The golden brand team idea was itself an example of PCH's willingness to experiment with organizational forms. It came from the smoking-cessation product Nicorette, which had been acquired a few years before. At its former company, Pharmacia, the Nicorette global marketing team had a long-standing practice of rapidly shifting spending in opportunistic ways. For instance, when someone famous died of lung cancer or a city banned smoking in public restaurants, Nicorette ads would suddenly appear in that locale. After the acquisition, when they saw how effective this team was, the PCH leaders "ring-fenced" it: letting the Nicorette marketers continue to operate with as few constraints as possible and observing them at work. Once they realized the value of this model, they rolled it out for all the golden brands.

For another capability, regulatory management, PCH set up a series of "communities of practice": formal working groups assigned to tap into the power of informal networks. The division leaders identified fifteen countries as key markets and, for each of them, named a group that included lawyers, health professionals, and a few representatives from the broader organization. These communities of practice could now help disseminate key practices and ideas from one country to another, relying heavily on respect, communication, and information, and bringing all of their professional insight and local knowledge to bear in managing regulatory issues.

A third structure was the designation of a vice president for global innovation. PCH needed a separate position to oversee pharmaceutical-like innovation, because the capability was so important, and because it was a new capability for this division. This vice president was responsible for green-lighting new projects, with a clear mandate to ensure that the company paid continual attention to the fit between R&D investment and the firm's overall way to play. This in turn enabled more risky ventures that paid off: for example, a campaign for portable, convenient health care.

All of these structures were new to Pfizer, and they made a tangible contribution to the success of the business.[1] At the same time, they were different from the matrix, network, or "czar" structures at most other companies, because they were organized directly around capabilities. When coherence is embedded in a hierarchical design, a great deal of frustration and wasted effort is avoided. For the first time at PCH, people did not have to choose between their functional priorities and their role in advancing the company's way to play. There were far fewer trade-offs between global and regional priorities, or between innovation and marketing; these mechanisms provided systematic ways to keep the management of capabilities at the center of everyone's attention, and to make that focus explicit.

Two factors in the PCH redesign made the greatest difference. The first was the spirit of relatively loose experimentation in designing structures that supported capabilities. The second was an emphasis on direct accountability. In most cases, to support capabilities systems and deliver high-quality performance, you need teams of people who can think on their feet, make decisions rapidly, and deliver results. Your goal in organization design, therefore, is to set up structures that promote accountability, independence, and cross-boundary connection.

Or as strategy writer Ken Favaro (coauthor of *The Three Tensions*) puts it, "The business unit structure should reflect the enterprise-wide strategy, not the other way around."[2] To keep everyone on course, rely on the innate coherence of the enterprise and the connection it gives people to your capabilities system and strategic priorities.

Coherence represents a great frontier in organization design. Already, a number of companies are experimenting with this. For example, as we saw in chapter 6, Ahlstrom divided its product lines into two basic clusters and set up different capabilities systems for these two groups, supporting them with a new organizational structure that focused the functional teams on enabling these capabilities. Some companies have set up accountable business units, with capability building and maintenance as part of their mandate. Others have put in place a "capabilities czar," someone with the responsibility for ensuring that the necessary investments are made and the right people are communicating. Other companies have initiated internal campaigns, in which the capability is given a name, top-level support, and perhaps a certification program for people who contribute their talents. Like PCH, some companies apply several of these approaches, each to a different capability.

Another model that could be useful for building capabilities is the nine company-wide cross-functional teams (CFTs) that Renault-Nissan CEO Carlos Ghosn set up in the early 2000s to provide a formal structure for implementing change. As Ghosn noted in an interview, the teams were deliberately set up to include "people from different geographies and different functions and different generations working together."[3] Each team was given accountability for a problem or a gap in capabilities at Renault-Nissan (such as product complexity, organizational structure, or business development) and came up with a plan to fix it within three months.[4] Today, the CFTs still exist across the organization, challenging the status quo and illuminating opportunities.

"In my experience," said Ghosn, explaining the importance of the CFTs and direct accountability, "executives in a company rarely reach across boundaries. Typically, engineers prefer solving problems with other engineers; salespeople like to work with fellow salespeople, and Americans feel more comfortable with other Americans. The trouble is that people working in the functional or regional teams tend not to ask themselves as many hard questions as they should."[5]

When you rethink your structures, any of these ideas (or others) might seem appropriate, but one principle should remain constant: make sure people are connected directly to outcomes related to your most relevant long-term distinctive capabilities, in addition to (or in place of) more short-term financial accountability. To accomplish this, you need to ensure that one feature is always present: measurable, recognizable outcomes that establish the progress people are making in developing and using the capabilities linked to your way to play.

For example, a team accountable for a capability involving innovation might track the financial returns linked to innovation investment, the yield curve, the freshness of the pipeline, the success rate, and the relationship of the innovation pipeline to the company's way to play.[6] These measures are all more meaningful than the typical figure of new-product sales.

You might argue that a structure already exists for building capabilities: the established functional organizations. These, after all, were created with the idea that professional specialists had specific know-how, to provide capabilities that contributed to a company's success. But as they have evolved in most companies, individual functions are almost never aligned to the kinds of capabilities systems that are needed for success. They are highly invested in functional excellence, as opposed to differentiating between distinctive capabilities and table stakes. Forcing them into the role of capabilities steward could lead to greater incoherence, especially if the tension between functional excellence and capabilities-oriented excellence is not recognized or managed.

Most organizations have a long way to go to build a truly capabilities-driven company, but we do see early signs of interest in a closer fit between organization and strategy. Some traditional functions may evolve this way; for example, research and development teams may be reorganized around the capabilities they support, rather than around their technological disciplines. Sales and marketing teams may meld together to drive demand in more coherent ways. This process may be accelerated as organizations grow tired of handoffs and infighting, and focus more on delivering value to customers. We even occasionally hear talk about replacing the traditional functions of a business—information technology, human resources, operations, and so on—with new departments, crossing traditional functions *and* product lines, directly responsible for building, maintaining, and deploying one of the distinctive capabilities within a system.

Conversations for Coherence

One critical part of developing coherence is setting a climate in which people are naturally moved to talk informally across boundaries: to coordinate mutual efforts, share information, and make sure that they are not working at cross-purposes. Thus, a major part of your initiative will concern fostering better conversations among your people. You can tap into what Jon Katzenbach, coauthor of *Leading Outside the Lines,* calls the "informal organization": the web of person-to-person connections through which people exchange knowledge and express commitment and pride.[7] These conversations are often seen as mere corridor talk, but they provide high-leverage ways to draw forth and develop the behaviors and attitudes of a coherent company.

To tap the informal organization, don't rely on highly orchestrated presentations or staff meetings. Instead, bring people together in unstructured conversations to talk through the issues raised by the changes you are making. These conversations might cover how the company expects to distinguish itself, whether the way to play makes sense, and how it fits with the jobs held by people in the room. Dialogues like this are helpful as long as they engage people and do not force or impose on them. These informal situations require light facilitation and a few ground rules (such as discouraging people from interrupting one another) to help everyone feel comfortable in the room.

Because their roles—and in some cases, their functions or business units—are at stake, people find it worthwhile to talk. Design the invitations so people from different functions and businesses meet. Capabilities are inherently cross-functional and cross-organizational, and these sessions will help people establish new working relationships across internal boundaries.

As part of its strategy initiative in the mid-2000s, Pfizer Consumer Healthcare conducted a series of such informal conversations among its top 150 managers. In each session, participants talked through the way to play that had been chosen, the capabilities they needed, and the processes that might change. To give the conversations a starting point and focus, while sparking attendees' imagination, Pfizer commissioned three elaborate, poster-sized illustrations and hung them on the meeting room walls. The first image was analogous to the current state of incoherence in the company (and the industry): a group of horse-drawn carriages, all moving in separate directions, represented the various PCH businesses. They were blocked by a roaring river that separated them from their chosen customers; those that dared try to cross were swept down the falls. The second image showed the state that PCH intended to be in soon: a group of better-maintained carriages, with healthier-looking horses, and a few automobiles. The six basic capabilities were portrayed, too, as pylons being placed across the rapids—and a few vehicles were beginning to cross. The third image was rendered as a blueprint, showing the bridge that PCH was building with its full-fledged capabilities system.

The 150 managers from that first conversation were, in turn, tasked with the mission of cascading these messages still further down the organization through similar informal efforts. To keep the messages consistent, they brought copies of the posters with them. The new approach was also summed up on a notebook-sized folding card that listed the products and services involved (labeled "aggressive and moderate growth brands") and that translated each of the capabilities into management imperatives (e.g., "Become the partner of choice for Rx-to-OTC switches"). Thereafter, both in the organized sessions and in the corridors and lunchrooms, one could hear the way to play and capabilities-based imperatives discussed and debated.

The most effective leaders we know conduct open discussion in just this way, modeling colloquy and coherence in their own behavior. They also look for informal champions of the new strategy, who understand its value and are interested in talking about the way to play, the new capabilities, and the changes they are making. They can be given more opportunities to step forward as pragmatic optimists, communicating across functions to help bring capabilities to life. The real value starts to accrue when people talk about this on their own accord. Setting up these conversations is like seeding a cloud to create the rain needed for a fertile organizational climate. An ongoing dialogue encourages people to live coherence every day.[8]

You will find this kind of network easier to maintain in a relatively coherent organization, where the structures, incentives, and informal networks are all aligned around the established way to play. People grow more used to communicating informally; they understand one another more easily, and the overall climate is less dysfunctional. Moreover, constant informal communication plays a critical role in building and maintaining capabilities, as people learn from one another. The interplay between coherence and personal connection is still not fully understood, but we believe that the experience of the next few years will make it clear how valuable they are to one another.

The Talent Opportunity

Consider all the decisions that a CEO has to make about people. Who is best suited for the organization? Which leadership characteristics and skills are best recruited, and which are best developed? How do we recruit and retain the right people and prepare them to lead?

One of the key roles for corporate headquarters is managing talent policies for the overall organization. This may be where the CEO and top management team have the greatest impact on the company in the long term; designing and implementing an innovative talent system is one of the most important things a leader can do to reinforce coherence.[9]

To implement an innovative talent system, you may need to change some deeply held views about human nature and the workplace. Many corporate leaders hold an image of a person's talent as aligned with their professional role or functional discipline: a finance manager will be oriented toward cutting costs while a marketer thinks of growth. But a coherent company, where many people work together across functions and businesses, requires people who fit well with that company's way to play. Individuals who would thrive working for an experience provider might feel stifled working for a consolidator, and vice versa.

Thus, you need a clear sense of the kind of people who fit into each part of your company: how forthright, deliberative, experimental, open to outsiders, fast-paced, risk-averse, respectful, or community-oriented they should be. What skills will they bring to make this capability succeed as part of a system—and do they understand how important that aspect of their job is? People who join your company should have the feeling that they were chosen and developed in line with its priorities— that they had earned a right to win in their jobs, just as the company had earned a right to win in the marketplace.

Brilliant individuals who don't represent a good fit for you will probably be worth more at another company, just as a business unit might be more profitable elsewhere if it doesn't fit your way to play. David Ulrich of the University of Michigan has something like this in mind when he writes about building "leadership brands": the type of leader who fits a retail chain might not be the right type of leader for a technology company.[10]

Fortunately, increased coherence makes it easier for companies to attract and retain high-quality talent. Applicants who fit are attracted because they know that their career prospects will be enhanced. Consider a public relations professional trying to decide between two offers. The first company, a small producer of packaged food, has told her that it wants a world-class PR department. But public relations is not relevant to that company's way to play; it will (and should) remain a table-stakes capability. There are only three PR professionals on staff, and they are scattered around the world; it's not enough to build a career path. The other offer comes from an innovative energy company whose way to play depends on R&D and establishing close relations with government and university research labs. It has a PR staff of seventy-five people that is recognized as one of the most influential teams in its profession. The applicant will have an opportunity to be mentored by some of those individuals and to carve out a future preparing messages about energy in emerging markets around the world. Which offer would you advise her to take?

In fact, given the realities of its capabilities system, the packaged-food company might be well advised to outsource the PR function altogether. Attracting and retaining talent will be tough for it, and without talent, the function may not even qualify as table stakes.

Research scientists know that going to work for Procter & Gamble, Pfizer, or 3M will improve their prospects. They will be working right at the heart of the company's capabilities system. They will be surrounded by other elite, skilled people who came to the company for the same reason. The company will be inclined to invest in their ideas and to give them chances to work on interesting projects. And they will have many opportunities to learn from each other and contribute.

Coherent companies also tend to place more emphasis on the support for talent—mentors, a clear development path, and recognition of the role people play in the company's capabilities system. Researchers such as Boris Groysberg of Harvard Business School have shown that the value of a star performer dramatically increases when he or she is supported by a network of other people—and, we would argue, by the formal and informal factors that help a network of people mesh well together, including the capabilities system itself.[11] Ken Favaro notes, "Your capabilities system is even more valuable than recruiting great people; it can make your people great."[12] In short, it's not just the individuals who differentiate a company; it's the company that differentiates the individuals, when it asks them to exercise their talent in a distinctive way.

In the next chapter, we'll look at that same capabilities system from a somewhat different perspective. We'll consider the view of the leader who has been responsible for initiating and overseeing this journey.

CHAPTER TWELVE

THE CAPABLE LEADER

In this book, we've made the case for coherence as the essential advantage of your company. We've illuminated the importance of mindfully choosing a way to play that is backed by a competitively differentiating and mutually reinforcing system of capabilities. And we've illustrated how companies align their product and service fit to these elements to create and sustain the right to win. We've looked at the process for a capabilities-driven strategy, the organizational changes that enable that strategy, and the approach you can take to growth, acquisitions, and expenses. There is one final ingredient critical to your success: your own coherent leadership.

One of our models of coherent leadership is former Procter & Gamble CEO A. G. Lafley, who is credited with driving P&G's remarkable performance comeback in the 2000s, and was (among many other honors) named the Academy of Management's Executive of the Year in 2007. But at the start of his tenure, he was not regarded with such acclaim. Indeed, Lafley has often spoken with humor about the stomach-lurching, 50 percent drop in the price of P&G stock the morning he was announced as CEO in March 2000:

> [It] was a loss of nearly $50 billion in market capitalization. P&G leaders were lying low. Heads were down. Competitors were on the attack. P&G business units were blaming headquarters, and headquarters was blaming business units. Employees were calling for heads to roll. Retirees—who had just lost half their retirement nest eggs—were madder than hatters. Analysts and investors were surprised and angry . . . After 15 days on the job, I lowered growth goals to what I felt was a realistic and sustainable level— and the stock dropped another $3.85![1]

Leaders on a journey to coherence will no doubt empathize. The path inevitably involves some similarly difficult moments, especially as people realize how much has to be cut back to keep the focus intact. Lafley describes P&G's remarkable comeback in terms of choice and persistence. "Most importantly," he told the Academy of Management in his award acceptance speech, "we've built discipline into the rhythm of the business. It's human nature to want to avoid choices. But strategy is all about choices. And making and sticking with those choices is the responsibility of leadership."

We agree. Your job, as a leader, is grounded in your ability to compel the organization to choose: to make choices yourself, to empower and teach others to choose, and to give them a framework with which to make better choices on an ongoing basis. Be willing, as Michael Porter puts it, "to teach others in the organization about strategy—and to say no."[2] If your organization like most, that won't be easy. It's natural for business-people to want to expand into adjacent markets, to extend their turf, to manage downside risks by hedging, and in general to stay unfocused. These instincts breed incoherence.

Capable leaders are neither confused nor confusing. They say "no" clearly to incoherent requests, and say "yes" even more clearly when they remind the organization what the destination looks like and the value of getting there. They know how to find the simplicity at the other side of complexity. Coherence becomes their greatest ally in articulating the logic for how the enterprise will win—and generating passion for getting there throughout the organization.

As a leader, you will have to be deliberate about the way you set and stick with your priorities. You have made hard choices about a way to play, the specific capabilities you will invest in, and the products and services that fit (and don't fit). You are forgoing growth opportunities that do not mesh with your capabilities system. Your whole company will reap great benefits from coherence, but perhaps not right away. You will need to make more tough decisions as you go along, and you will be compelled to set an example of "living coherently" over the following months and years. Your own behavior will inevitably become a model for the alignment of strategy and execution that you wish to see around you.

The same is true for the other senior leaders of your company: help your direct reports see why changing their own behavior is important. Some of them may no longer have core roles now that the rules have changed, and you may need to find ways to bring them on board, give them new positions, or encourage them to go elsewhere. Leaders tell us surprisingly often that the hardest part of their job is managing their relations with other senior people; they feel caught between the desire to empower others and the temptation of seizing the reins and making most of the strategic decisions themselves. This conflict itself may be a sign of incoherence; without a clear way to play and a common sense of what adds value, most top managers will naturally pursue conflicting priorities. Conversely, when the destination is advertised and the path to it is evident, people embark on the journey willingly and with clarity, and the results achieved are orders of magnitude greater.

As we said in chapter 3, Mahatma Gandhi's famous quote, "We need to be the change we wish to see in the world," can be your starting point for change.[3] People will look to you to stand by and sustain the commitment you have made. Focus on the opportunities that you know will produce results. Be careful not to appear as if you are hedging your bets. If you don't have the visceral confidence that you are on a good path, then you may not be on the right journey, because it's very easy to be seduced by nagging doubts into the kind of incoherence that undermines the whole effort.

There may be times, of course, when the results you expect aren't forthcoming (although in our experience, this doesn't happen very often). Something may be wrong with your strategic choice or, more likely, with your execution (such as the development of your capabilities system) or with your time frame. Don't suddenly shift gears; rather, explore the reasons why things have gone sour, establish a rationale for what you will do next, and shift in a way that preserves your focus. Make sure people always know where the company is going and why, and that you are still committed to the goals of creating value and establishing your essential advantage.

The same kind of clarity is needed when you communicate your strategy—inside or outside the company. Build your case on a clear and logically consistent framework. You're going to have a different story to tell—to Wall Street, to your board, to regulators, to employees, to union leaders if you have them, and to all other constituents. Explicitly talk about your company's way to play, the market where you compete, your goals, and the capabilities system that will support those goals.

You don't have to be a great communicator to lead a capabilities-driven strategy, as long as you can talk clearly. Learn to distill your directives into simple, direct statements of your intent. Most organizations betray their incoherence in the way people talk. If you are clear about your strategy and direction and consistent in the way you operate, these attributes will be more important than charisma. Establish practices, incentives, and discussions that help your company's people move toward coherence. Don't organize the process by yourself; convene a working group (the core team, as described in chapter 10), and broaden that group as the scale of your efforts expands. When people see sustainable success, you won't have difficulty recruiting them to this effort; they'll want to be associated with it.

John Barth, the former chairman and CEO of Johnson Controls, Inc. (JCI), is another model of leadership. For many years, he was a steady hand in moving his company toward coherence. In the early 1980s, he joined the firm as part of its acquisition of Hoover Universal (the auto seat business). At that time, JCI was a sleepy business with $300 million in annual revenues.[4] Barth and the rest of the JCI leadership team turned it into a powerhouse components company, generating more than $34 billion annually by the time he retired as chairman and CEO at the end of 2007.[5]

JCI's direction was rooted in foresight: in a solid understanding that the auto industry in Detroit and Japan was changing. Cars and trucks were getting more complex, and components manufacturers would have to compensate. Barth and his colleagues took the necessary steps ahead of time to divest businesses that no longer fit (such as plastics) and invest more in the capabilities that they would need.

As he focused on this strategy, Barth cultivated lieutenants, enlisting their support in leading the whole organization forward. Acting as a counselor to all, he treated them individually with discretion and varying degrees of bottom-line responsibility. In 1996, when JCI bought Prince, a highly regarded auto interior design company, Barth made a point of identifying and retaining Prince's best managers. As a result, the JCI–Prince deal is recognized as one of the few successful mergers in post–World War II automotive history.

Capable leaders, like Lafley, Barth, and many others, are inspiring. They have learned to generate excitement and inspiration in a world of ruthless choice. Their own jobs become more enjoyable. They are not deluged by disjointed, ad hoc events. They have the enviable role of leading a group of purposeful, creative people who are used to winning in the marketplace and who understand why they are successful. When they go, they leave behind a company that is stronger, more capable, and more coherent than it was before; a company with a solid way to play and a capabilities system that enables people to grow; a company that is primed to create value, wealth, and quality of life for decades to come. In business, this is the most powerful legacy.

NOTES

Chapter 1

1. "Driving an Ambitious Change Program at Pfizer Consumer Health Care," in Gregg Bangs and Jim Reisler, eds., *Booz Allen Hamilton Professional Excellence Awards 2002* (McLean, VA: Booz Allen Hamilton, 2002); and supporting documentation for the award.

2. Michael Porter, "What is Strategy?" *Harvard Business Review,* November–December 1996, 61–78.

3. C. K. Prahalad and Gary Hamel, "The Core Competence of the Corporation," *Harvard Business Review*, May–June 1990, 79–91.

4. Kim Warren, "Capability-Based Strategy: Beware Core Competencies," Talking About Strategy with Kim Warren, Web page, December 14, 2008, www.kimwarren.com.

5. Andrew S. Grove, *Only the Paranoid Survive: How to Exploit the Crisis Points That Challenge Every Company* (New York: Doubleday, 1996).

6. Walter Kiechel III, *The Lords of Strategy: The Secret Intellectual History of the New Corporate World* (Boston: Harvard Business Press, 2010), 5–6.

Chapter 2

1. The Coca-Cola Company Web site, www.thecoca-colacompany.com.

2. A. G. Lafley, "What Only the CEO Can Do," *Harvard Business Review*, May 2009; and Roger Martin, *The Design of Business: Why Design Thinking Is the Next Competitive Advantage* (Boston: Harvard Business School Press, 2009), chapter 4.

3. A. G. Lafley with Ram Charan, "P&G's Innovation Culture," *strategy+business*, Autumn 2008.

4. Lafley, "What Only the CEO Can Do."

Notes

5. Steven Wheeler, Walter McFarland, and Art Kleiner, "A Blueprint for Strategic Leadership," *strategy+business,* Winter 2007.

6. James B. Shein and Loredana Yamada, "Sara Lee: A Tale of Another Turnaround," Case 5-108-009 (KEL353) (Evanston, IL: Kellogg School of Management, 2008).

7. "Sara Lee to Sell Personal Care Brands to Unilever," *Reuters,* September 25, 2009; Brenda Barnes and Marcel Smits, Sara Lee, presentation to the Consumer Analyst Group of New York, February 16, 2010.

8. Arie P. de Geus, "Planning as Learning," *Harvard Business Review,* March–April 1988, 70–74.

9. Gary Hamel and C. K. Prahalad, *Competing for the Future* (Boston: Harvard Business School Press, 1994), 205–206.

10. C. K. Prahalad and Gary Hamel, "The Core Competence of the Corporation," *Harvard Business Review,* May–June 1990, 79–91.

11. Michael Porter, "The Five Competitive Forces That Shape Strategy," *Harvard Business Review,* January 2008, 78–93.

12. Jürgen Ringbeck and Daniel Röska, "Flying Through Stormy Skies: How Airlines Can Navigate the Global Recession," Booz & Company white paper, New York, 2009.

13. Jeremiah McNichols, "The True Story of Pampers Dry Max, Part 1: The Diaper Wars," *Z Recommends,* May 15, 2010, www.zrecommends.com/detail/the-true-story-of-pampers-dry-max-part-1-the-diaper-wars/.

14. Marcus Morawietz, Matthias Bäumier, Pedro Caruso, and Jayant Gotpagar, *Future of Chemicals III: The Commoditization of Specialty Chemicals, Managing the Inevitable,* Booz & Company white paper, New York, 2010.

15. Pankaj Ghemawat, *Redefining Global Strategy* (Boston: Harvard Business School Press, 2007), 27.

16. Gerald Adolph, Justin Pettit, and Michael Sisk, *Merge Ahead: Mastering the Five Enduring Trends of Artful M&A* (New York: McGraw-Hill, 2009), 70–77.

17. Alfonso Martinez and Ronald Haddock, "The Flatbread Factor," *strategy+business,* Spring 2007.

18. Edward Tse, *The China Strategy: Harnessing the Power of the World's Fastest-Growing Economy* (New York: Basic Books, 2010), 1–2; Kristian Foden-Vencil, "Chinese Sportswear Company Opens U.S. Store," February 23, 2010, *Morning Edition,* NPR, February 23, 2010, transcript available at http://www.npr.org/templates/story/story.php?storyId=123993826.

19. Andrew Dunn and Suresh Seshadri, "Motorola Accuses Huawei of Conspiring to Steal Trade Secrets," *BusinessWeek,* July 22, 2010.

20. Richard Fletcher, "Turtles and Toads Boost Tesco," *Sunday Times,* March 5, 2006. http://business.timesonline.co.uk/tol/business/article737485.ece.

21. Tse, *The China Strategy,* 51.

22. Alexander V. Izosimov, "Managing Hypergrowth," *Harvard Business Review,* April 2008, 121–127.

23. Ann Graham, "Too Good to Fail: The Tata Group," *strategy+business,* Spring 2010.

24. Judd Kahn and Bruce C. Greenwald, *Competition Demystified* (New York: Portfolio, 2005), 368; Noel Tichy and Stratford Sherman, *Control Your Destiny or Someone Else Will* (New York: HarperBusiness, 2001), 96.

25. Tichy and Sherman, *Control Your Destiny or Someone Else Will,* 83.

26. Claudia H. Deutsch, "A Chairman's Fall: GE Magic Can Fade, After GE," *New York Times,* January 4, 2007; Brian Hindo, "At 3M, A Struggle Between Efficiency and Creativity," *BusinessWeek*, June 11, 2007.

Chapter 3

1. Paul Branstad and Chuck Lucier, "Zealots Rising: The Case for Practical Visionaries," *strategy+business,* 1st Quarter, 2001.

2. Jeffrey Schwartz, Douglas Lennick, and Pablo Gaito, "That's the Way We Do Things Around Here," *strategy+business*, Spring 2011.

3. Mahatma Gandhi, quoted in Michel W. Potts, "Arun Gandhi Shares the Mahatma's Message," *India—West* 27, no. 13 (February 1, 2002): A34; and Mahatma Gandhi, indirectly quoted by Arun Gandhi, in Carmella B'Hahn, "Be the Change You Wish to See: An Interview with Arun Gandhi," *Reclaiming Children and Youth* 10, no. 1 (spring 2001): 6.

Chapter 4

1. Reference for Business, *Encyclopedia of Business,* 2nd ed., s.v. "Walmart Stores, Inc."; www.referenceforbusiness.com/businesses/M-Z/Walmart-Stores-Inc.html.

2. Michael Barbara, "It's Not Only About Price at WalMart," *New York Times,* March 2, 2007; John R. Wells and Travis Haglock, "The Rise of Wal-Mart Stores Inc. 1962–1987," Case 9-707-439 (Boston: Harvard Business School, 2008); P. Fraser Johnson, "Supply Chain Management at Wal-Mart," Case 907D01 (London, ON: Richard Ivey School of Buisness, 2006); Stephen P. Bradley and Pankaj Ghemawat, "Wal-Mart Stores, Inc.," Case 9-794-024 (Boston: Harvard Business School, 2002); Meg Marco et al, "Leaks: Walmart Powerpoint on '3 Consumer' Plan," *The Consumerist*, March 6, 2007, http://consumerist.com/2007/03/leaks-walmart-powerpoint-on-3-customer-plan.html; George Stalk, Jr., Philip Evans, and Lawrence E. Shulman, "Competing on Capabilities: The New Rules of Corporate Strategy," *Harvard Business Review*, March–April 1992.

3. Mike Duff, "Why Walmart Should Be Worried: Target's Cheap Chic Is Hitting the Bulls-Eye," BNET, April 29, 2010; http://industry.bnet.com/retail/10009247/target-streaks-past-walmart-driven-by-cheap-chic-revival/.

4. Sears Holdings Corporation, "About Kmart" Web page; http://www.sears holdings.com/about/kmart/.

5. Harry Cunningham, quoted in James Champy and Nitin Nohria, *The Arc of Ambition* (New York: Basic, 2000), 69.

6. Gary Hamel and C. K. Prahalad, *Competing for the Future* (Boston: Harvard Business School Press, 1994; paperback edition 1996), 141.

7. Theodore Kinni, "What Experience Would You Like with That?", *strategy+business,* Autumn 2010. The six books are: B. Joseph Pine II and James H. Gilmore, *The Experience Economy: Work Is Theatre and Every Business a Stage* (Boston: Harvard Business School Press, 1999); Bernd H. Schmitt, *Experiential Marketing: How to Get Customers to Sense, Feel, Think, Act, and Relate to Your Company and Brands* (New York: Free Press, 1999); Lewis P. Carbone, *Clued In: How to Keep Customers Coming Back Again and Again* (London: FT Press, 2004); Leonard L. Berry and Kent D. Seltman, *Management Lessons from Mayo Clinic: Inside One of the World's Most Admired Service Organizations* (New York: McGraw-Hill, 2008); Lior Arussy, *Customer Experience Strategy: The Complete Guide from Innovation to Execution* (New York: 4i, 2010); and Jeanne Bliss, *Chief Customer Officer: Getting Past Lip Service to Passionate Action* (San Francisco: Jossey-Bass, 2006).

8. Joe Wilcox, "Remembering Apple's First Store," eWeek AppleWatch, May 15, 2008; http://blogs.eweek.com/applewatch/content/channel/remembering_apples_first_store.html.

9. Michael Porter, "The Five Competitive Forces That Shape Strategy," *Harvard Business Review,* January 2008, 78–93; Theodore Levitt, "Marketing Myopia," *Harvard Business Review*, July/August 1960, 45–56.

10. Clayton M. Christensen, *The Innovator's Dilemma: When New Technologies Cause Great Firms to Fail* (Boston: Harvard Business School Press, 1997).

Chapter 5

1. W. Brian Arthur, "Increasing Returns and the New World of Business," *Harvard Business Review,* July 1996, 100–109.

2. Thomas A. Stewart and Julia Kirby, "The Institutional Yes: An Interview with Jeff Bezos," *Harvard Business Review,* October 2007, 74–82.

3. Gary Hamel and C. K. Prahalad, *Competing for the Future* (Boston: Harvard Business School Press, 1994; paperback edition 1996), 199.

4. Edward Tse, *The China Strategy: Harnessing the Power of the World's Fastest-Growing Economy* (New York: Basic Books, 2010), 137–138.

5. Alfred D. Chandler, Jr., *Inventing the Electronic Century* (New York: Free Press, 2001), 5.

6. Alfred D. Chandler, Jr., *Shaping the Industrial Century: The Remarkable Story of the Evolution of the Modern Chemical and Pharmaceutical Industries*

(Boston: Harvard University Press, 2005), 9; Art Kleiner, "Professor Chandler's Revolution," *strategy+business,* 2nd Quarter 2002.

7. Walter Kiechel III, "Seven Chapters of Strategic Wisdom," *strategy+business,* Spring 2010.

8. Chandler, *Inventing the Electronic Century,* 87–90 and 96–97.

9. Kaj Grichnik and Conrad Winkler, *Make or Break: How Manufacturers Can Make the Leap from Decline to Revitalization* (New York: McGraw-Hill, 2008), 1–4.

Chapter 6

1. Lyla Adwan, "The Breath Strips Revolution," *EuroMonitor International,* May 23, 2003; www.euromonitor.com/The_breath_strips_revolution.

2. Nat Ives, "Quirky Campaigns Vie for the Growing Market in Breath Strips, No Longer a One-Brand Novelty," *New York Times,* May 27, 2003; "Best Inventions 2002," *Time,* www.time.com/time/2002/inventions/med_breath.html.

3. Jane Larson, "Wrigley's Big Play: The Breath Strip," *Phoenix Arizona Republic,* February 23, 2003.

4. Adwan, "The Breath Strips Revolution; It's on the Tip of Your Tongue," *BusinessWeek,* July 31, 2006, http://www.businessweek.com/magazine/content/06_31/b3995059.htm; "Breath Strip Downturn Prompts Wrigley Production Changes," *Food Production Daily,* October 22, 2004, www.foodproductiondaily.com/Processing/Breath-strip-downturn-prompts-Wrigley-production-changes; and Wrigley, "Wrigley Brands Woven into the Fabric of Everyday Life," company Web page; www.wrigley-trade.co.uk/index.cfm?articleid=190.

5. Walter Kiechel, *The Lords of Strategy: The Secret Intellectual History of the New Corporate World* (Boston: Harvard Business Press, 2010), chapter 2.

6. Harry Quarls, Thomas Pernsteiner, and Kasturi Rangan, "Love Your Dogs," *strategy+business,* Spring 2006.

7. Kiechel, *The Lords of Strategy,* 68.

Chapter 7

1. David Fairlamb and Laura Cohn, "A Bumpy Ride in Europe," *BusinessWeek,* October 6, 2003.

2. Reuters, "In-Store Clinics Boost Wal-Mart's Health," May 30, 2007.

3. Ann Zimmerman, "Retail Sales Show Signs of Life," *Wall Street Journal,* March 6, 2009.

4. Christopher Zook, *Profit from the Core: A Return to Growth in Turbulent Times* (Boston: Harvard Business Press, 2010), chapter 5.

5. John Varley, "Barclay's Global Acceleration," *strategy+business,* Summer 2007.

6. Robert Manor, "Busch Closing Eagle Snacks, but Rival Frito-Lay to Buy 4 of 5 Plants," *St. Louis Post-Dispatch,* February 8, 1996.

7. Richard Melcher, "How Anheuser's Eagle Became Extinct," *BusinessWeek,* March 4, 1996, 68.

8. Ibid.

9. Chris Dettro, "Is Frito-Lay Getting Overly Shelf-ish? Competition Tactics Called into Question," *The Springfield (IL) State Journal-Register,* June 1, 1996; Mark L. Sirower, "Imagined Synergy: A Prescription for a No-Win Deal," *Mergers & Acquisitions,* January–February 1998.

10. Ibid.

11. "P&G Buys Eagle Snacks Brand Name," *New York Times,* May 7, 1996, D4.

12. Melcher, "How Anheuser's Eagle Became Extinct."

13. W. Chan Kim and Renée Mauborgne, *Blue Ocean Strategy* (Boston: Harvard Business School Press, 2005).

14. Randall Stross, "Failing Like a Buggy Whip Maker? Better Check Your Simile," *New York Times,* January 9, 2010.

15. Matthew Egol, Harry Hawkes, and Greg Springs, "Reinventing Print Media," *strategy+business*, Autumn 2009; and David Dobson, "Integrated Innovation at Pitney Bowes," *strategy+business*, Winter 2009.

16. Gerald Adolph and Justin Pettit, *Merge Ahead: Mastering the Five Enduring Trends of Artful M&A* (New York: McGraw-Hill, 2009), 20.

Chapter 8

1. Bob Hutchens and Justin Pettit, "Deal or No Deal? Outcomes from a Decade of Healthcare M&A," working paper, Booz & Company, New York, September 22, 2009.

2. Gerald Adolph, Justin Pettit, and Michael Sisk, *Merge Ahead: Mastering the Five Enduring Trends of Artful M&A* (New York: McGraw-Hill, 2009), 36–38.

3. Jonathan Wheatley, "Shares Soar As Brazilian Banks Merge," London, *Financial Times,* November 3, 2008.

4. Pallavi Gogoi, "A Bittersweet Deal for Wrigley," *BusinessWeek,* May 1, 2008.

5. Dean Best, "Mars, Wrigley Look to a Sweeter Future," Just-food.com, April 29, 2008, http://www.just-food.com/analysis/mars-wrigley-look-to-a-sweeter-future_id102165.aspx.

Chapter 9

1. Vinay Couto, Ashok Divakaran, Mahadeva Matt Mani, and Cheri Lantz, "Survival vs. Success: How Companies Are Responding to the Recession, and Why It's Not Enough," Booz & Company white paper, March 26, 2009.

Notes

2. James H. Keyes, "Letter to Shareholders" (Milwaukee, WI: Johnson Controls, Inc. Annual Report, 1995), 2.

3. *Lehman Brothers Industry Report* (New York: Lehman Brothers, October 1995).

4. "R.J. Reynolds Professional Excellence Award," in *Booz Allen Hamilton Annual Report* (New York: Booz Allen Hamilton, 2004).

Chapter 10

1. William Duggan, "How Aha Really Happens," *strategy+business*, Spring 2011.

2. George S. Day, "Is It Real? Can We Win? Is It Worth Doing? Managing Risk and Reward in an Innovation Portfolio," *Harvard Business Review*, December 2007, 110–120.

3. Noel Tichy and Stratford Sherman, *Control Your Destiny or Someone Else Will* (New York: HarperBusiness, 2001), 113.

Chapter 11

1. PCH Growth of 8 percent in 2005 versus industry growth of 4 percent, from the supporting documentation to: "Driving an Ambitious Change Program at Pfizer Consumer Health Care," in Gregg Bangs and Jim Reisler, eds., *Booz Allen Hamilton Professional Excellence Awards 2002* (McLean, VA: Booz Allen Hamilton, 2002).

2. Ken Favaro, interview with authors, October 19, 2009.

3. Carlos Ghosn, quoted in Gary Neilson and Bruce Pasternack, *Results: Keep What's Good, Fix What's Wrong, and Unlock Great Performance* (New York: Crown Business, 2005), 227.

4. Carlos Ghosn, "Saving the Business Without Losing the Company," *Harvard Business Review*, January 2002, 37–45.

5. Ibid.

6. For more on the idea of tracking financial returns and investment in innovation, see Alexander Kandybin, "Which Innovation Efforts Will Pay?" *Sloan Management Review*, Fall 2009.

7. Jon Katzenbach and Zia Khan, *Leading Outside the Lines: How to Mobilize the (in)Formal Organization, Energize Your Team, and Get Better Results* (San Francisco: Jossey-Bass, 2010).

8. Ibid., chapter 1.

9. DeAnne Aguirre, Laird Post, and Sylvia Ann Hewlett, "The Talent Innovation Imperative," *strategy+business*, Autumn 2009.

Notes

10. Dave Ulrich and Norm Smallwood, *Leadership Brand: Developing Customer-Focused Leaders to Drive Performance and Build Lasting Value* (Boston, Harvard Business School Press, 2007).

11. Jeffrey Pfeffer, "Are There Stars in Banking—or Anywhere Else?" August 5, 2009, BNET, http://blogs.bnet.com/ceo/?p=2611.

12. Ken Favaro, interview with authors, October 19, 2009.

Chapter 12

1. A. G. Lafley, "Ongoing Transformation: Leading Change to Sustain Growth and Leadership" (transcript of speech given to Academy of Management, Philadelphia, August 5, 2007).

2. Michael Porter, "What Is Strategy?" *Harvard Business Review,* November–December 1996, 61–78.

3. Mahatma Gandhi, quoted in Michel W. Potts, "Arun Gandhi Shares the Mahatma's Message," *India—West* 27, no. 13 (February 1, 2002): A34; and Mahatma Gandhi, indirectly quoted by Arun Gandhi, in Carmella B'Hahn, "Be the Change You Wish to See: An Interview with Arun Gandhi," *Reclaiming Children and Youth* 10, no. 1 (spring 2001): 6.

4. Paul Branstad and Chuck Lucier, "Zealots Rising: The Case for Practical Visionaries," *strategy +business,* 1st Quarter 2001.

5. "Johnson Controls Elects Stephen Roell Chief Executive Officer; John M. Barth to Retire After 38 Years of Service," Auto Channel Web site, July 26, 2007, www.theautochannel.com/news/2007/07/26/056247.html.

BIBLIOGRAPHY

Books

Adolph, Gerald, Justin Pettit, and Michael Sisk. *Merge Ahead: Mastering the Five Enduring Trends of Artful M&A*. New York: McGraw-Hill, 2009.

Baghai, Mehrdad, Stephen Coley, and David White. *The Alchemy of Growth*. London: Orion Business, 1999.

Banerji, Shumeet, Paul Leinwand, and Cesare R. Mainardi. *Cut Costs and Grow Stronger: A Strategic Approach to What to Cut and What to Keep*. Boston: Harvard Business Press, 2009.

Champy, James, and Nitin Nohria. *The Arc of Ambition: Defining the Leadership Journey*. New York: Basic Books, 2000.

Chandler, Alfred D., Jr. *Inventing the Electronic Century: The Epic Story of the Consumer Electronics and Computer Industries*. New York: Free Press, 2001.

_____. *Shaping the Industrial Century: The Remarkable Story of the Evolution of the Modern Chemical and Pharmaceutical Industries*. Boston: Harvard University Press, 2005.

Christensen, Clayton M. *The Innovator's Dilemma: When New Technologies Cause Great Firms to Fail*. Boston: Harvard Business School Press, 1997.

Collins, Jim. *How the Mighty Fall: And Why Some Companies Never Give In*. New York: HarperCollins, 2009.

Dodd, Dominic, and Ken Favaro. *The Three Tensions: Winning the Struggle to Perform Without Compromise*. San Francisco: Jossey-Bass, 2007.

Ghemawat, Pankaj. *Redefining Global Strategy: Crossing Borders in a World Where Differences Still Matter*. Boston: Harvard Business School Press, 2007.

Grichnik, Kaj, Conrad Winkler, and Jeffrey Rothfeder. *Make or Break: How Manufacturers Can Make the Leap from Decline to Revitalization*. New York: McGraw-Hill, 2008.

Bibliography

Groysberg, Boris. *Chasing Stars: The Myth of Talent and the Portability of Performance.* Princeton, NJ: Princeton University Press, 2010.

Hamel, Gary, and C. K. Prahalad. *Competing for the Future.* Boston: Harvard Business School Press, 1994.

Joni, Saj-Nicole, and Damon Beyer. *The Right Fight: How Great Leaders Use Healthy Conflict to Drive Performance, Innovation, and Value.* New York: HarperBusiness, 2010.

Kahn, Judd, and Bruce C. Greenwald. *Competition Demystified: A Radically Simple Approach to Business Strategy.* New York: Portfolio, 2005.

Katzenbach, Jon R. *Why Pride Matters More Than Money: The Power of the World's Greatest Motivational Force.* New York: Crown Business, 2003.

Katzenbach, Jon R., and Zia Khan. *Leading Outside the Lines: How to Mobilize the (in)Formal Organization, Energize Your Team, and Get Better Results.* San Francisco: Jossey-Bass, 2010.

Kiechel, Walter. *The Lords of Strategy: The Secret Intellectual History of the New Corporate World.* Boston: Harvard Business Press, 2010.

Kim, W. Chan, and Renée Mauborgne. *Blue Ocean Strategy: How to Create Uncontested Market Space and Make the Competition Irrelevant.* Boston: Harvard Business School Press, 2005.

Kleiner, Art. *The Age of Heretics: A History of the Radical Thinkers Who Reinvented Corporate Management.* San Francisco: Jossey-Bass, 2008.

Martin, Roger. *The Design of Business: Why Design Thinking Is the Next Competitive Advantage.* Boston: Harvard Business School Press, 2009.

Moeller, Leslie H., Edward C. Landry, and Theodore Kinni. *The Four Pillars of Profit-Driven Marketing: How to Maximize Creativity, Accountability, and ROI.* New York: McGraw-Hill, 2009.

Neilson, Gary, and Bruce Pasternack. *Results: Keep What's Good, Fix What's Wrong, and Unlock Great Performance.* New York: Crown Business, 2005.

Nonaka, Ikijuro, and Hirotaka Takeochi. *The Knowledge-Creating Company: How Japanese Companies Create the Dynamics of Innovation.* New York: Oxford University Press, 1995.

Senge, Peter, Art Kleiner, Charlotte Roberts, Richard Ross, and Bryan Smith. *The Fifth Discipline Fieldbook: Strategies and Tools for Building a Learning Organization.* New York: Doubleday, 1994.

Spiegel, Eric, Neil McArthur, and Rob Norton. *Energy Shift: Game-Changing Options for Fueling the Future.* New York: McGraw-Hill, 2009.

Tichy, Noel, and Stratford Sherman. *Control Your Destiny or Someone Else Will.* New York: HarperBusiness, 2001.

Tse, Edward. *The China Strategy: Harnessing the Power of the World's Fastest-Growing Economy.* New York: Basic Books, 2010.

Bibliography

Ulrich, Dave, and Norm Smallwood. *Leadership Brand: Developing Customer-Focused Leaders to Drive Performance and Build Lasting Value.* Boston: Harvard Business School Press, 2007.

Vollmer, Christopher, and Geoffrey Precourt. *Always On: Advertising, Marketing, and Media in an Era of Consumer Control.* New York: McGraw-Hill, 2008.

Zook, Chris. *Unstoppable: Finding Hidden Assets to Renew the Core and Fuel Profitable Growth.* Boston: Harvard Business School Press, 2007.

Zook, Chris, and James Allen. *Profit from the Core: A Return to Growth in Turbulent Times.* Boston: Harvard Business Press, 2010.

Articles

Aguirre, DeAnne, Laird Post, and Sylvia Ann Hewlett. "The Talent Innovation Imperative." *strategy+business,* Fall 2009, 38–49.

Arthur, W. Brian. "Increasing Returns and the New World of Business." *Harvard Business Review,* July 1996, 100–109.

Branstad, Paul, and Chuck Lucier. "Zealots Rising: The Case for Practical Visionaries." *strategy+business,* 1st Quarter 2001, 42–53.

Ghosn, Carlos. "Saving the Business Without Losing the Company." *Harvard Business Review,* January 2002, 37–45.

Graham, Ann. "Too Good to Fail: The Tata Group." *strategy+business,* Spring 2010, 62–73.

Izosimov, Alexander V. "Managing Hypergrowth." *Harvard Business Review,* April 2008, 121–127.

Kandybin, Alexander. "Which Innovation Efforts Will Pay?" *Sloan Management Review,* Fall 2009, 53–60.

Kiechel, Walter. "Seven Chapters of Strategic Wisdom." *strategy+business,* Spring 2010, 93–99.

Kinni, Theodore. "What Experience Would You Like with That?" *strategy+business,* Fall 2010, 96–100.

Kleiner, Art. "Professor Chandler's Revolution." *strategy+business,* 2nd Quarter 2002, 84–91.

Lafley, A. G. "What Only the CEO Can Do." *Harvard Business Review,* May 2009, 54–62.

Lafley, A. G., and Ram Charan. "P&G's Innovation Culture." *strategy+business,* Autumn 2008, 40–49.

Martinez, Alfonso, and Ronald Haddock. "The Flatbread Factor." *strategy+business,* Spring 2007, 66–79.

Nath, Deepika, and D. Sudharshan. "Measuring Strategy Coherence Through Patterns of Strategic Choices." *Strategic Management Journal* 15, no. 1 (January 1994): 43–61.

Bibliography

Porter, Michael E. "What is Strategy?" *Harvard Business Review,* November–December 1996, 61–78.

Porter, Michael E. "The Five Competitive Forces That Shape Strategy." *Harvard Business Review,* January 2008, 78–93.

Prahalad, C. K., and Gary Hamel. "The Core Competence of the Corporation." *Harvard Business Review,* May–June 1990, 79–91.

Quarls, Harry, Thomas Pernsteiner, and Kasturi Rangan. "Love Your Dogs." *strategy+business,* Spring 2006, 58–65.

Stewart, Thomas A., and Julia Kirby. "The Institutional Yes: An Interview with Jeff Bezos." *Harvard Business Review,* October 2007, 74–82.

Varley, John. "Barclay's Global Acceleration." *strategy+business,* Summer 2007, 16–17.

INDEX

Note: Page numbers followed by *f* refer to figures; page numbers followed by *t* refer to tables.

ABOUT THE AUTHORS

PAUL LEINWAND is a Partner in Booz & Company's global consumer, media, and retail practice. He advises clients on the topics of strategy and capability building and has coauthored a number of works on capabilities-driven strategy, including the book *Cut Costs and Grow Stronger* (with Shumeet Banerji and Cesare Mainardi, Harvard Business Press) and several articles in *Harvard Business Review* and *strategy+business*. He also serves as chair of the firm's Knowledge and Marketing Advisory Council. Mr. Leinwand earned a bachelor's degree in political science from Washington University and a master's degree in management with distinction from the Kellogg Graduate School of Management.

CESARE MAINARDI is Managing Director of Booz & Company's North American business and a member of the firm's Executive Committee. He has served as global leader of its worldwide functional, consumer products, and health practices. Mr. Mainardi is a coauthor of *Cut Costs and Grow Stronger* and several articles on business strategy published in *Harvard Business Review* and *strategy+business*. Since joining Booz & Company in 1986, he has worked with large global companies to help them achieve major business transformations, typically through multiyear strategy-based efforts spanning functions and geographies. *Consulting* magazine named him to its list of the Top 25 Consultants in 2005. He holds a master's in management from the Kellogg Graduate School of Management and a master's in manufacturing engineering from Northwestern, where he was awarded a Whirlpool Fellowship in Manufacturing.